D1167558

SOLO

SOLO

NAVPRESS

NAVPRESS ◯.

NavPress is the publishing ministry of The Navigators, an international Christian organization and leader in personal spiritual development. NavPress is committed to helping people grow spiritually and enjoy lives of meaning and hope through personal and group resources that are biblically rooted, culturally relevant, and highly practical.

For a free catalog go to www.NavPress.com
or call 1.800.366.7788 in the United States or 1.800.839.4769 in Canada.

Black: 978-1-60006-672-6
Brown: 978-1-61521-533-1

Cover design by Burnkit

Devotional text by Jan Johnson, J. R. Briggs, and Katie Peckham.

Published in association with the literary agency of Alive Communications, Inc., 7680 Goddard Street, Suite 200, Colorado Springs, CO 80920, www.alivecommunications.com.

Printed in China

2 3 4 5 6 7 8 / 14 13 12 11 10

INTRODUCTION TO *SOLO*

The devotional you hold is unique. It isn't designed to teach you to study the Bible but rather to develop a conversation between you and God. The devotions found in *Solo* are based on the classical method of lectio divina: reading, thinking, praying, and living Scripture with the intention of inviting an infinite, omniscient God into your life — as it is, no gloss, no veneer. Lectio divina is more Bible basking than Bible study, as it teaches you to absorb and meditate on Scripture, to converse with God openly, and to live out what has become a part of you — his Word.

But it's not easy. Lectio divina takes practice, and lots of it. You will have to learn to be quiet, to silence the voices of responsibility, self, family, and even religion in order to hear what God has to say to you. Try not to view the elements of lectio divina as steps to be checked off your to-do list. Instead, allow them to meld together in the intentional process of listening to God, of focusing on him and learning what he would have from you and for you, his beloved. Don't worry if no lightning strikes or brilliant revelations come. Sometimes devotion means just sitting in the presence of God.

We know the four elements of lectio divina as Read, Think, Pray, and Live. Each element has a purpose, but don't be surprised if they overlap and weave into each other. Remember as you dive into this devotional that lectio divina is about wholeness: whole practice, whole Bible, whole God.

Read. Thoughtfully, leisurely, faithfully — read the epic love story that is the Bible. Yes, love story. The Bible is the chronicle of God's love for his people from the darkness before Eden to eternity with him in heaven. You are in it; I am in it. But most important, God is in it. Here you will meet him face-to-face.

Eugene Peterson called the Bible "a book that reads us even as we read it." That's an uncommon sort of book, and it requires an uncommon sort of read. Knowing facts about God doesn't change your relationship with him, so take the time to splash around in the Word, to absorb it, to discover what God has to say to you each day.

In each *Solo* devotion, you will find a Scripture passage, but also a reference to an expanded passage. I encourage you to read them both, slowly, attentively, and repeatedly. As Peterson said, "The Bible is given to us in the first place simply to invite us to make ourselves at home in the world of God . . . and become familiar with the way God speaks and the ways in which we answer him with our lives." No Scripture passage exists in a vacuum. Whenever you can, take the time to stretch beyond the passage put before you to understand the larger context in which it is found. The more you read, the more you will understand about yourself and this God who created you.

Think. Each subtle, significant, powerful word of Scripture is meant for you. One word may speak today and another tomorrow, but God sent each of them straight into your life. So listen. Go into your reading with a clean slate. Don't bring what you think you need to hear, what others have said, or what you've been taught about a particular passage. Don't bring fear that you'll misinterpret the text. This is about what God has to say to you.

Our lives are full of static. Whether it's our to-do list, our emotions, or just plain noise, it can be hard to sift God's voice from all the racket. By meditating on each word, by turning it over and over in your mind, you will discover that, as God himself is infinitely complex, so his thoughts have subtle meaning beyond the rote. The more you think about what you read, the more familiar you will become with his voice.

Pray. God yearns to converse with you. And he wants far more than just "thanks for this, can I please have that" prayer. Respond to him in dialogue. That means it's as much about listening as it is about speaking. Open your ears and your heart to hear his voice. Sing praises or laments; write your thoughts in a journal; dance or prostrate yourself before him. Pray.

Maybe God has challenged you. Tell him how you feel, but always remember that what he asks, he asks for your good. He is loving and merciful, not manipulative and harsh. If you come across something in your reading that you don't understand, tell him about it. Ask him about it. Fill your prayers with Scripture. Using the words you have read helps you ensure that your prayers line up with God's Word and intention for your life.

It's easy for us in our culture of doing to want to skim over this part. Don't. Even if you are quiet and he is quiet, you are learning to communicate with God.

Live. You can read, think, and pray all day, but unless you live in God's Word as well, you miss the point. The Bible says, "Isn't it obvious that

God-talk without God-acts is outrageous nonsense?" (James 2). If you have taken God's Word to heart and truly made it part of you, it will by its very nature change you. And when it does, you will find yourself called to act. There will come a time when God takes you to the end of yourself then asks you to go further. He wants you to put yourself at his disposal, to go and do what he asks, even the impossible. When that time comes, you will need the Word he has seared on your heart to give you comfort and strength. This is the "more and better life than they ever dreamed of" of which Jesus spoke (John 10).

///

Solo. One on one. Just you and God.

This book is designed to help you develop the habit of lectio divina. For those of you new to the discipline, several of the devotions are specifically intended to help you begin what may become a lifelong pursuit. They are each marked with a ☯. Also, though lectio divina emphasizes becoming familiar with God's whole Word, rather than focusing on any particular part, there may be times when you need to hear God's voice on a specific issue. For those times we have provided an index of topics that will guide you to a devotion that may be just what you need.

The *Solo* devotions are tailored to help you learn to listen to what God may want to say to you through his Word. You will find that every seventh day is marked as a day of reflection, a time to sit back and let God guide your thoughts and prayers back to themes and Scripture from the previous week. Don't be afraid to reflect, and don't be afraid to go back. Each time you read these devotions, you may find that God has something new to say, for though he is the same always, you change a little each day as he shapes you into the person he designed you to be.

And so begins the journey.

TO THE READER

If there is anything distinctive about *The Message*, perhaps it is because the text is shaped by the hand of a working pastor. For most of my adult life I have been given a primary responsibility for getting the message of the Bible into the lives of the men and women with whom I worked. I did it from pulpit and lectern, in home Bible studies and at mountain retreats, through conversations in hospitals and nursing homes, over coffee in kitchens and while strolling on an ocean beach. *The Message* grew from the soil of forty years of pastoral work.

As I worked at this task, this Word of God, which forms and transforms human lives, did form and transform human lives. Planted in the soil of my congregation and community, the seed words of the Bible germinated and grew and matured. When it came time to do the work that is now *The Message*, I often felt that I was walking through an orchard at harvest time, plucking fully formed apples and peaches and plums from laden branches. There's hardly a page in the Bible I did not see lived in some way or other by the men and women, saints and sinners, to whom I was pastor — and then verified in my nation and culture.

I didn't start out as a pastor. I began my vocational life as a teacher and for several years taught the biblical languages of Hebrew and Greek in a theological seminary. I expected to live the rest of my life as a professor and scholar, teaching and writing and studying. But then my life took a sudden vocational turn to pastoring in a congregation.

I was now plunged into quite a different world. The first noticeable difference was that nobody seemed to care much about the Bible, which so recently people had been paying me to teach them. Many of the people I worked with now knew virtually nothing about it, had never read it, and weren't interested in learning. Many others had spent years reading it but for them it had gone flat through familiarity, reduced to clichés. Bored, they dropped it. And there weren't many people in between. Very few were interested in what I considered my primary work, getting the words of the Bible into their heads and hearts, getting the message lived. They found newspapers and magazines, videos and pulp fiction more to their taste.

Meanwhile I had taken on as my life work the responsibility of getting these very people to listen, really listen, to the message in this book. I knew I had my work cut out for me.

I lived in two language worlds, the world of the Bible and the world of Today. I had always assumed they were the same world. But these people didn't see it that way. So out of necessity I became a "translator" (although I wouldn't have called it that then), daily standing on the border between two worlds, getting the language of the Bible that God uses to create and save us, heal and bless us, judge and rule over us, into the language of Today that we use to gossip and tell stories, give directions and do business, sing songs and talk to our children.

And all the time those old biblical languages, those powerful and vivid Hebrew and Greek originals, kept working their way underground in my speech, giving energy and sharpness to words and phrases, expanding the imagination of the people with whom I was working to hear the language of the Bible in the language of Today and the language of Today in the language of the Bible.

I did that for thirty years in one congregation. And then one day (it was April 30, 1990) I got a letter from an editor asking me to work on a new version of the Bible along the lines of what I had been doing as a pastor. I agreed. The next ten years was harvest time. *The Message* is the result.

The Message is a reading Bible. It is not intended to replace the excellent study Bibles that are available. My intent here (as it was earlier in my congregation and community) is simply to get people reading it who don't know that the Bible is read-able at all, at least by them, and to get people who long ago lost interest in the Bible to read it again. But I haven't tried to make it easy — there is much in the Bible that is hard to understand. So at some point along the way, soon or late, it will be important to get a standard study Bible to facilitate further study. Meanwhile, read in order to live, praying as you read, "God, let it be with me just as you say."

— EUGENE H. PETERSON

LIVE BEFORE GOD

MATTHEW 5:27-29,33-37

27-28 "You know the next commandment pretty well, too: 'Don't go to bed with another's spouse.' But don't think you've preserved your virtue simply by staying out of bed. Your *heart* can be corrupted by lust even quicker than your *body*. Those leering looks you think nobody notices — they also corrupt.

29 "Let's not pretend this is easier than it really is. If you want to live a morally pure life, here's what you have to do: You have to blind your right eye the moment you catch it in a lustful leer. You have to choose to live one-eyed or else be dumped on a moral trash pile. . . .

33-37 "And don't say anything you don't mean. This counsel is embedded deep in our traditions. You only make things worse when you lay down a smoke screen of pious talk, saying, 'I'll pray for you,' and never doing it, or saying, 'God be with you,' and not meaning it. You don't make your words true by embellishing them with religious lace. In making your speech sound more religious, it becomes less true. Just say 'yes' and 'no.' When you manipulate words to get your own way, you go wrong."

READ

Read the passage aloud slowly.

THINK

Imagine yourself going to the mailbox today and finding in it a letter addressed to you, containing the words of this passage. Think of yourself opening the letter. Then read the passage aloud again, and as you do, see yourself walking back from the mailbox.

1. What meaning do the words have for you? What is Jesus getting at?
2. How do you "pretend this is easier than it really is" regarding having a pure thought life? Regarding really meaning what you say?
3. How do these commands speak to the deepest part of you, the part Jesus wants?

PRAY

Ask Jesus to show you situations in which you are likely to say something you don't mean. Ask him to help you discover what that's about — perhaps impressing people or pretending to be better than you are.

LIVE

Jesus understands how difficult his words are for us. Sense yourself being pulled along with love and grace by Jesus.

PRAY WITH SIMPLICITY

MATTHEW 6:5-13

5 "And when you come before God, don't turn that into a theatrical production either. All these people making a regular show out of their prayers, hoping for stardom! Do you think God sits in a box seat?

6 "Here's what I want you to do: Find a quiet, secluded place so you won't be tempted to role-play before God. Just be there as simply and honestly as you can manage. The focus will shift from you to God, and you will begin to sense his grace.

7-13 "The world is full of so-called prayer warriors who are prayer-ignorant. They're full of formulas and programs and advice, peddling techniques for getting what you want from God. Don't fall for that nonsense. This is your Father you are dealing with, and he knows better than you what you need. With a God like this loving you, you can pray very simply. Like this:

Our Father in heaven,
Reveal who you are.
Set the world right;
Do what's best —
    as above, so below.
Keep us alive with three square meals.
Keep us forgiven with you and forgiving others.
Keep us safe from ourselves and the Devil.
You're in charge!
You can do anything you want!
You're ablaze in beauty!
    Yes. Yes. Yes."

READ

Read the passage aloud slowly, noticing what it says about simple prayer versus complex, showy prayer. What is the most important issue for you listed below? Be honest.

Simple Prayer	Complex, Showy Prayer
finding a quiet, secluded place	turning prayer into a dramatic production
not role-playing before God	making a regular show of prayers
being with God as simply and honestly as you can	using formulas, programs, and advice
watching the focus shift from you to God	using techniques to get what you want from God

THINK

Read the passage again. This time, picture yourself sitting with other people about six feet from Jesus and listening as he says these words. When does Jesus look directly at you as he teaches? What words is he saying because he knows you need them? Why are those words meant for you?

PRAY

Paraphrase the Lord's Prayer (verses 9-13). In other words, add to or change each phrase in a way that makes the prayer specific to you.

LIVE

Sit quietly before God, praying the Lord's Prayer if you wish, or just being silent. Feel the focus shift from you to God. Enjoy that.

2

AN INVITATION

MATTHEW 9:9-13

9   Passing along, Jesus saw a man at his work collecting taxes. His name was Matthew. Jesus said, "Come along with me." Matthew stood up and followed him.

10-11   Later when Jesus was eating supper at Matthew's house with his close followers, a lot of disreputable characters came and joined them. When the Pharisees saw him keeping this kind of company, they had a fit, and lit into Jesus' followers. "What kind of example is this from your Teacher, acting cozy with crooks and riffraff?"

12-13   Jesus, overhearing, shot back, "Who needs a doctor: the healthy or the sick? Go figure out what this Scripture means: 'I'm after mercy, not religion.' I'm here to invite outsiders, not coddle insiders."

READ

Once you are in a quiet place, thank God for the gift of his Word. Then read the passage.

THINK

When have you felt like the outsider? When have people scrutinized and criticized you for the people you associated with? Do you think their judgment was fair? Why or why not?

Ponder these words from Jesus: "'I'm after mercy, not religion.' I'm here to invite outsiders, not coddle insiders." Where do you think Jesus was going with this statement?

If you were present that day, how might have you responded?

PRAY

Hold your hands open in front of you. Sit in silence for several moments, staring at them. Invite the Holy Spirit to guide your life today. Pray that your hands will be a physical representation of what you desire your heart to be. Acknowledge that you are a physical open invitation to the Holy Spirit for his guidance toward paths of mercy, not religiosity. Ask him to bring to mind outsiders to whom you can show mercy today.

LIVE

As you are reminded of God's mercy on your life, take the risk of showing mercy to outsiders.

JESUS THE HEALER

MATTHEW 9:18-26

18-19 As he finished saying this, a local official appeared, bowed politely, and said, "My daughter has just now died. If you come and touch her, she will live." Jesus got up and went with him, his disciples following along.

20-22 Just then a woman who had hemorrhaged for twelve years slipped in from behind and lightly touched his robe. She was thinking to herself, "If I can just put a finger on his robe, I'll get well." Jesus turned — caught her at it. Then he reassured her: "Courage, daughter. You took a risk of faith, and now you're well." The woman was well from then on.

23-26 By now they had arrived at the house of the town official, and pushed their way through the gossips looking for a story and the neighbors bringing in casseroles. Jesus was abrupt: "Clear out! This girl isn't dead. She's sleeping." They told him he didn't know what he was talking about. But when Jesus had gotten rid of the crowd, he went in, took the girl's hand, and pulled her to her feet — alive. The news was soon out, and traveled throughout the region.

READ

Read the passage.

THINK/PRAY

Pick the episode that is more striking to you — either the healing of the hemorrhaging woman or the raising of the official's daughter. (If you choose the first story, read Leviticus 15:25-30 now to better understand her situation.)

Read the passage again, carefully. Immerse yourself in the story as though you are a character in it — an observer or one named in the passage. Use every sense to enter the scene; take part in each moment. Where are you in relation to others? To Jesus? What is it like for you to be there? How are you feeling?

After you exit the scene, talk with Jesus about what you saw and experienced.

LIVE

Think about your experience in the scene, as well as your discussion with Jesus, and jot down anything you want to remember.

Put your pen aside and sit quietly for a few minutes. Listen to the sound of your own breathing and the silence.

End by saying the Lord's Prayer aloud: "Our Father in heaven, reveal who you are. Set the world right; do what's best — as above, so below. Keep us alive with three square meals. Keep us forgiven with you and forgiving others. Keep us safe from ourselves and the Devil. You're in charge! You can do anything you want! You're ablaze in beauty! Yes. Yes. Yes" (Matthew 6:9-13).

● WALK WITH ME

MATTHEW 11:28-30

28-30   "Are you tired? Worn out? Burned out on religion? Come to me. Get away with me and you'll recover your life. I'll show you how to take a real rest. Walk with me and work with me — watch how I do it. Learn the unforced rhythms of grace. I won't lay anything heavy or ill-fitting on you. Keep company with me and you'll learn to live freely and lightly."

READ
Read the passage slowly.

THINK
Read the passage again, listening for the words or phrases that stand out to you, such as:

- "come to me"
- "recover your life"
- "real rest"
- "walk with me and work with me"
- "watch how I do it"
- "keep company with me"

Notice the many different ways Jesus says, "Hang out with me." Which one do you find most inviting? Why?

What would it feel like to walk with Jesus and work with him? It's okay to be honest; "freely and lightly" may not describe what you think it would really be like. Instead you might think it would be forced and difficult. If so, what would you *desire* for it to be like?

Have you feared that a walk with Jesus might require heavy or ill-fitting things? What are they?

PRAY
Jesus speaks very personally and conversationally in this passage, using phrases like "Come to me." In fact, *I* or *me* occurs eight times, and *you* occurs five times. So consider that Jesus has been talking to *you*. What is your reply? What do you need to discuss with Jesus today?

LIVE

Walk with Jesus, either in your mind or on an actual walk. As you do, turn these words from Jesus over in your mind: rest, unforced, keep company with me, freely, lightly.

EYES SCREWED SHUT

MATTHEW 13:10-17

10 The disciples came up and asked, "Why do you tell stories?"

11-15 He replied, "You've been given insight into God's kingdom. You know how it works. Not everybody has this gift, this insight; it hasn't been given to them. Whenever someone has a ready heart for this, the insights and understandings flow freely. But if there is no readiness, any trace of receptivity soon disappears. That's why I tell stories: to create readiness, to nudge the people toward receptive insight. In their present state they can stare till doomsday and not see it, listen till they're blue in the face and not get it. I don't want Isaiah's forecast repeated all over again:

> Your ears are open but you don't hear a thing.
> Your eyes are awake but you don't see a thing.
> The people are blockheads!
> They stick their fingers in their ears
> so they won't have to listen;
> They screw their eyes shut
> so they won't have to look,
> so they won't have to deal with me face-to-face
> and let me heal them.

16-17 "But you have God-blessed eyes—eyes that see! And God-blessed ears—ears that hear! A lot of people, prophets and humble believers among them, would have given anything to see what you are seeing, to hear what you are hearing, but never had the chance."

READ

Read the passage carefully.

THINK

Notice what Jesus says about human hearts. What does he draw attention to about our receptivity to his message? How does he deal with our resistance? What does he want for us?

Now read Jesus' words again, and hear them as if he is saying them to you personally. Meditate on his words until the message becomes familiar. What stands out that relates to your life?

PRAY

Tell Jesus about your meditation — your thoughts and feelings. Listen for his response.

LIVE

Search your memory (or your journal) for any insights God has given you in recent weeks as you have interacted with his Message. What have those truths led you to do? Were there times when God invited you to act on or think about something, but you ignored the request or put it off? Why? Revisit that experience with Jesus. Remember that his greatest desire is not to get you to act a certain way but to engage with you in relationship.

DAY 7

GOD ENCOUNTERS

On this seventh day, review and reflect on all you have read this week. Take the time to revel in the ways you've encountered God in the past six days.

A MATTER OF THE HEART

MATTHEW 15:1-14

1-2   After that, Pharisees and religion scholars came to Jesus all the way from Jerusalem, criticizing, "Why do your disciples play fast and loose with the rules?"

3-9   But Jesus put it right back on them. "Why do you use your rules to play fast and loose with God's commands? God clearly says, 'Respect your father and mother,' and, 'Anyone denouncing father or mother should be killed.' But you weasel around that by saying, 'Whoever wants to, can say to father and mother, What I owed to you I've given to God.' That can hardly be called respecting a parent. You cancel God's command by your rules. Frauds! Isaiah's prophecy of you hit the bull's-eye:

> These people make a big show of saying the right thing,
>> but their heart isn't in it.
> They act like they're worshiping me,
>> but they don't mean it.
> They just use me as a cover
>> for teaching whatever suits their fancy."

10-11   He then called the crowd together and said, "Listen, and take this to heart. It's not what you swallow that pollutes your life, but what you vomit up."

12   Later his disciples came and told him, "Did you know how upset the Pharisees were when they heard what you said?"

13-14   Jesus shrugged it off. "Every tree that wasn't planted by my Father in heaven will be pulled up by its roots. Forget them. They are blind men leading blind men. When a blind man leads a blind man, they both end up in the ditch."

READ

Sit at a table with this devotional. Read this passage with your palms open as a way of communicating that you are open to hear from God.

THINK

Jesus seems to spend a lot of time provoking the Pharisees by speaking harshly to them. Of all the religious groups in Israel, Jesus rebukes the Pharisees the most. And yet, these are supposed to be the most devout leaders in the entire nation. Joining Jesus in bashing the Pharisees is tempting. Thinking *I'm glad I'm not like them* is easy. But we often resemble the Pharisees more than we'd like to admit.

Think back and identify a time when your heart responded to Jesus the way the Pharisees responded to him. What might help you identify the moments when your heart is more Pharisee-like than Jesus-like? Who can you invite to help keep your heart in check?

Ponder the words Matthew quotes from Isaiah (verses 8-9). Under what circumstances does this describe you? What do you think God wants you to do about it?

PRAY

Ask God to give you a Jesus-like heart, one that is humble, transparent, and genuine.

LIVE

Invite others to help you keep your heart in check by giving them permission to ask you tough heart questions.

THE SOFTENED HEART

MATTHEW 19:3-9

3   One day the Pharisees were badgering him: "Is it legal for a man to divorce his wife for any reason?"

4-6   He answered, "Haven't you read in your Bible that the Creator originally made man and woman for each other, male and female? And because of this, a man leaves father and mother and is firmly bonded to his wife, becoming one flesh — no longer two bodies but one. Because God created this organic union of the two sexes, no one should desecrate his art by cutting them apart."

7   They shot back in rebuttal, "If that's so, why did Moses give instructions for divorce papers and divorce procedures?"

8-9   Jesus said, "Moses provided for divorce as a concession to your hard-heartedness, but it is not part of God's original plan. I'm holding you to the original plan, and holding you liable for adultery if you divorce your faithful wife and then marry someone else. I make an exception in cases where the spouse has committed adultery."

READ

Read the passage aloud slowly. Consider that this teaching is an example Jesus gave from a longer teaching about forgiveness.

THINK

Matthew recorded this to come just after Jesus tells the parable about the servant who is forgiven a great deal and cannot forgive someone who has harmed him only slightly.

Imagine that you are there as Jesus is teaching. You've heard his parable about the unforgiving servant, and now he speaks of people being hardhearted. As you read the passage again, consider that we divorce ourselves from people in many ways — leaving a church, leaving a project, leaving a friendship. (If you wish, read Matthew 18:23-35 or try to recall the parable of the unforgiving servant. Try to feel for yourself that servant's incredible hardheartedness.)

1. What is hardheartedness really about?
2. How does hardheartedness toward others violate God's will for all of us?
3. Where in your life is hardheartedness a problem?
4. What is God urging you to do to cultivate a softened heart?

PRAY

Ask God to bring to mind those who might want to plead with you, "Give me a chance" (see Matthew 18:26,29). Try to picture yourself having mercy on this person. If it seems impossible, ask God to pour out his love into your heart.

LIVE

Sit quietly before God. Become hardhearted — how does this feel in your body? Become softhearted — how does that feel in your body? Stay with the softheartedness for several minutes.

DAY 10
EXPANDED PASSAGE: MATTHEW 21:1-17

JESUS THREW THEM OUT

MATTHEW 21:12-17

12-14 Jesus went straight to the Temple and threw out everyone who had set up shop, buying and selling. He kicked over the tables of loan sharks and the stalls of dove merchants. He quoted this text:

My house was designated a house of prayer;
You have made it a hangout for thieves.

Now there was room for the blind and crippled to get in. They came to Jesus and he healed them.

15-16 When the religious leaders saw the outrageous things he was doing, and heard all the children running and shouting through the Temple, "Hosanna to David's Son!" they were up in arms and took him to task. "Do you hear what these children are saying?"

Jesus said, "Yes, I hear them. And haven't you read in God's Word, 'From the mouths of children and babies I'll furnish a place of praise'?"

17 Fed up, Jesus turned on his heel and left the city for Bethany, where he spent the night.

READ

Read the passage aloud.

THINK/PRAY

Imagine you are there when Jesus comes in the temple and cleanses it. To get your imagination going, read the passage a second time, but then set this book aside, close your eyes, and see yourself as a part of the scene.

Who are you? Where are you? Smell the incense and the scent of burning, sacrificed animal flesh. Jump at the loud crash of the tables and the fury in Jesus' voice as the sounds echo in the stunned silence. What are the expressions on the faces around you?

Now let the blind and crippled come into your view. Watch Jesus healing them. Listen to the voices of the children as they play and shout, "Hosanna!" What's your reaction to them? To Jesus' interaction with the disabled? To the indignation of the religious leaders? (Include not only your mental reaction but your physical reaction too, if any.)

Now follow Jesus as he walks out of the city, still fuming. Picture him initiating a conversation with you about the events of the day. Imagine that he asks you what it was like. Tell him.

LIVE

In C. S. Lewis's *The Lion, the Witch and the Wardrobe,* the lion, Aslan, "isn't safe. But he's good."[1]

Consider this statement in light of what you've just read about Jesus. How does this view of Jesus — that he sometimes does things that are painful to us — alter your perception of who he is? In what ways does this affect how you relate to him?

OVERLOOKED AND IGNORED

MATTHEW 25:31-40

31-33 "When he finally arrives, blazing in beauty and all his angels with him, the Son of Man will take his place on his glorious throne. Then all the nations will be arranged before him and he will sort the people out, much as a shepherd sorts out sheep and goats, putting sheep to his right and goats to his left.

34-36 "Then the King will say to those on his right, 'Enter, you who are blessed by my Father! Take what's coming to you in this kingdom. It's been ready for you since the world's foundation. And here's why:

> I was hungry and you fed me,
> I was thirsty and you gave me a drink,
> I was homeless and you gave me a room,
> I was shivering and you gave me clothes,
> I was sick and you stopped to visit,
> I was in prison and you came to me.'

37-40 "Then those 'sheep' are going to say, 'Master, what are you talking about? When did we ever see you hungry and feed you, thirsty and give you a drink? And when did we ever see you sick or in prison and come to you?' Then the King will say, 'I'm telling the solemn truth: Whenever you did one of these things to someone overlooked or ignored, that was me — you did it to me.'"

READ

Read the passage aloud slowly. As you read it, understand that Jesus said these words aloud too. They are his words.

THINK

This is a part of an entire sermon (or thematic sermon series) on watchfulness (see Matthew 23–25). The people in this passage were watching for the needy, but they didn't know it was Jesus they were watching. Read the passage again silently and slowly.

1. What words or phrases stand out to you?
2. Who are the overlooked and ignored in your life?
3. Imagine yourself overlooked and ignored. What do you now have in common with Jesus?
4. In what ways is God asking you to give someone food, drink, a room, clothes; to stop and visit someone; to go to a person locked away physically, emotionally, or mentally?

PRAY

Ask Jesus how he exists in the overlooked and ignored. Ponder this mystery. Ask him to show you your next step in grasping some part of this.

LIVE

As you serve people who are overlooked and ignored, be mindful of the presence of Jesus. See if you can spot him.

MY GOD, WHY?

MATTHEW 27:45-54

45-46   From noon to three, the whole earth was dark. Around mid-afternoon Jesus groaned out of the depths, crying loudly, *"Eli, Eli, lama sabach-thani?"* which means, "My God, my God, why have you abandoned me?"

47-49   Some bystanders who heard him said, "He's calling for Elijah." One of them ran and got a sponge soaked in sour wine and lifted it on a stick so he could drink. The others joked, "Don't be in such a hurry. Let's see if Elijah comes and saves him."

50   But Jesus, again crying out loudly, breathed his last.

51-53   At that moment, the Temple curtain was ripped in two, top to bottom. There was an earthquake, and rocks were split in pieces. What's more, tombs were opened up, and many bodies of believers asleep in their graves were raised. (After Jesus' resurrection, they left the tombs, entered the holy city, and appeared to many.)

54   The captain of the guard and those with him, when they saw the earthquake and everything else that was happening, were scared to death. They said, "This has to be the Son of God!"

READ

If you have time, read Matthew 26:31–27:56. If not, read the shorter passage.

THINK

Church historian Bruce Shelley wrote, "Christianity is the only major religion to have as its central event the humiliation of its God."[2] Consider not only that Jesus' humiliation is immense, but his anguish is deeper than we can imagine. His own people wildly demanded his death. His friends deserted him. And now even his intimately loving Father has turned away.

Spend time wrestling heart and mind with why the Almighty would choose such a path. Reread Jesus' own words a few times to get closer to his experience.

PRAY

What wells up inside you as you spend time with the paradox of Jesus' death? Wonder? Grief? Distractedness? Tell Jesus about what surfaces. Then gently pull your thoughts back to his sacrifice and death, reading the passage again if you need to. Allow yourself to sink into the event deeply, again being aware of your reaction and talking to Jesus about it.

LIVE

Find a new place to be silent. For example, walk in a quiet place or sit in an empty church sanctuary. Bring your wristwatch or PDA and set the alarm so you can forget the time until it reminds you. Meditate on Jesus' sacrifice for you, then wait for what he would have you receive from him.

PARALYZED AND DESPERATE

MARK 2:1-12

1-5   After a few days, Jesus returned to Capernaum, and word got around that he was back home. A crowd gathered, jamming the entrance so no one could get in or out. He was teaching the Word. They brought a paraplegic to him, carried by four men. When they weren't able to get in because of the crowd, they removed part of the roof and lowered the paraplegic on his stretcher. Impressed by their bold belief, Jesus said to the paraplegic, "Son, I forgive your sins."

6-7   Some religion scholars sitting there started whispering among themselves, "He can't talk that way! That's blasphemy! God and only God can forgive sins."

8-12   Jesus knew right away what they were thinking, and said, "Why are you so skeptical? Which is simpler: to say to the paraplegic, 'I forgive your sins,' or say, 'Get up, take your stretcher, and start walking'? Well, just so it's clear that I'm the Son of Man and authorized to do either, or both . . ." (he looked now at the paraplegic), "Get up. Pick up your stretcher and go home." And the man did it — got up, grabbed his stretcher, and walked out, with everyone there watching him. They rubbed their eyes, incredulous — and then praised God, saying, "We've never seen anything like this!"

READ

Ask a friend or family member to read the verses aloud to you. Close your eyes and listen intently.

THINK

Imagine yourself in the story, referring to the text again as much as you need to. For a few minutes each, place yourself in the skins of the different individuals. Consider yourself on the roof with the four friends and the paralytic. Become the crippled man on the mat. Think of yourself as one of the four friends. Imagine yourself as someone standing in the crowded room of the house, able to easily see and hear the Pharisees. And consider yourself the owner of the house.

With which person in the story do you identify the most? Why?

PRAY

Imagine yourself again as the paralytic lying on his stretcher. Jesus looks at you and says, "Son, I forgive your sins." What is the expression on his face? What is the tone of his voice? What are you feeling when you hear those words?

Talk to Jesus about his actions and your reactions — mental, emotional, physical, spiritual.

LIVE

Consider those people around you who need a life-altering interaction with Jesus. What might you need to do to bring them to the feet of Jesus, even if it means making a big sacrifice for them?

DAY 14

GOD ENCOUNTERS

On this seventh day, review and reflect on all you have read this week. Take the time to revel in the ways you've encountered God in the past six days.

TELLING YOUR WHOLE STORY

MARK 5:25-34

25-29   A woman who had suffered a condition of hemorrhaging for twelve years — a long succession of physicians had treated her, and treated her badly, taking all her money and leaving her worse off than before — had heard about Jesus. She slipped in from behind and touched his robe. She was thinking to herself, "If I can put a finger on his robe, I can get well." The moment she did it, the flow of blood dried up. She could feel the change and knew her plague was over and done with.

30   At the same moment, Jesus felt energy discharging from him. He turned around to the crowd and asked, "Who touched my robe?"

31   His disciples said, "What are you talking about? With this crowd pushing and jostling you, you're asking, 'Who touched me?' Dozens have touched you!"

32-33   But he went on asking, looking around to see who had done it. The woman, knowing what had happened, knowing she was the one, stepped up in fear and trembling, knelt before him, and gave him the whole story.

34   Jesus said to her, "Daughter, you took a risk of faith, and now you're healed and whole. Live well, live blessed! Be healed of your plague."

READ
Read the passage aloud slowly.

THINK
Read the passage again, putting yourself in the place of the woman. (If it helps to imagine yourself instead as a man with an oozing sore, that's fine.)

1. From where did you get the courage to come behind Jesus and touch his clothes?
2. When Jesus looks at you, how do you feel?
3. How does it feel for you to tell Jesus your story — and for him to listen so well? (Read in the expanded passage how he also listens well when he has a little girl to heal.)
4. How does it feel to be complimented publicly by this holy man?

PRAY
Tell Jesus the "whole story" about something that's troubling you. Kneel as the woman did. Let the eyes of Jesus rest on you and bless you.

LIVE
Get up from your kneeling position and then sit or stand. Close your eyes and sense that you are living well, living blessed.

TAKE YOUR TURN

MARK 7:24-30

24-26   From there Jesus set out for the vicinity of Tyre. He entered a house there where he didn't think he would be found, but he couldn't escape notice. He was barely inside when a woman who had a disturbed daughter heard where he was. She came and knelt at his feet, begging for help. The woman was Greek, Syro-Phoenician by birth. She asked him to cure her daughter.

27   He said, "Stand in line and take your turn. The children get fed first. If there's any left over, the dogs get it."

28   She said, "Of course, Master. But don't dogs under the table get scraps dropped by the children?"

29-30   Jesus was impressed. "You're right! On your way! Your daughter is no longer disturbed. The demonic affliction is gone." She went home and found her daughter relaxed on the bed, the torment gone for good.

READ

Read the expanded passage to get the big picture in which this incident occurs. As you do, identify with Jesus' disciples: Witness his amazing miracles. Feel the exhaustion of not even having time to eat. See the people constantly pressing in on all sides.

Now reread the shorter passage. What is your reaction to the Greek woman's request? How do you feel when Jesus initially turns her down? When he changes his mind?

THINK

Pause to allow the Holy Spirit to help you understand what your initial reactions tell you about your heart.

Then take a moment to look more closely at this woman. What tensions, concerns, and frustrations fill her daily life? What do you see in her face when she's told to "stand in line"? When she replies? What does she feel when she sees her healed daughter?

Maybe at the end of this meditation you see things in a new light. In what ways does your new perspective mingle with your first reaction?

PRAY/LIVE

Become aware of Jesus in the room with you now, inviting you to talk with him about what today's passage was like for you. Don't hide feelings and thoughts that have surfaced within you, but openly share with him any questions, frustrations, or concerns you have. What does Jesus want you to see today? What does he want you to know? Spend several minutes in silence considering what you've experienced.

HEARTSTRINGS

MARK 10:17-22

17   As he went out into the street, a man came running up, greeted him with great reverence, and asked, "Good Teacher, what must I do to get eternal life?"

18-19   Jesus said, "Why are you calling me good? No one is good, only God. You know the commandments: Don't murder, don't commit adultery, don't steal, don't lie, don't cheat, honor your father and mother."

20   He said, "Teacher, I have — from my youth — kept them all!"

21   Jesus looked him hard in the eye — and loved him! He said, "There's one thing left: Go sell whatever you own and give it to the poor. All your wealth will then be heavenly wealth. And come follow me."

22   The man's face clouded over. This was the last thing he expected to hear, and he walked off with a heavy heart. He was holding on tight to a lot of things, and not about to let go.

READ

Pick a pace and read this passage quickly. Read it again at a different pace. Did you notice anything different the second time?

THINK

Write down your thoughts about this story. How are you similar to the rich man? How are you different?

Jesus knows that, though the rich man is morally good, he still has strings attached to his heart that will keep him from being a devoted follower.

Take an internal inventory of your heart. What things are deeply attached to your heart that must be relinquished for you to be a whole-hearted follower of Jesus? They may be possessions, but they may also be thoughts, relationships, activities, and so on.

Later in the passage, Jesus says this about anyone's chance of getting into God's kingdom: "No chance at all if you think you can pull it off by yourself. Every chance in the world if you let God do it" (verse 27). Based on these words from Jesus, write in your own words a description of the grace God offers to each one of us.

PRAY

Reflect on God's grace. Thank God for the grace he extends to you. Confess the times when you have abused his grace. Offer God the strings of your heart, those that keep you from completely following Jesus. Ask God to help you sever those strings and replace them with fray-proof connections to him.

LIVE

Live in freedom and follow Jesus.

THE BIG PICTURE

MARK 12:28-34

28 One of the religion scholars came up. Hearing the lively exchanges of question and answer and seeing how sharp Jesus was in his answers, he put in his question: "Which is most important of all the commandments?"

29-31 Jesus said, "The first in importance is, 'Listen, Israel: The Lord your God is one; so love the Lord God with all your passion and prayer and intelligence and energy.' And here is the second: 'Love others as well as you love yourself.' There is no other commandment that ranks with these."

32-33 The religion scholar said, "A wonderful answer, Teacher! So lucid and accurate — that God is one and there is no other. And loving him with all passion and intelligence and energy, and loving others as well as you love yourself. Why, that's better than all offerings and sacrifices put together!"

34 When Jesus realized how insightful he was, he said, "You're almost there, right on the border of God's kingdom."

After that, no one else dared ask a question.

READ

Read the passage aloud slowly.

THINK

Put yourself in the place of the religion scholar. You have studied theology and can explain its intricate details. You are weary with how most scholars argue over minor issues. You've come to Jesus to ask him to give you the big picture. Read the passage again, letting Jesus answer you directly.

Be impressed with Jesus' answer: He has combined part of the often-repeated *Shema Israel* (see Deuteronomy 6:4-9) and the last part of a much less quoted command: "Don't seek revenge or carry a grudge against any of your people. Love your neighbor as yourself. I am GOD" (Leviticus 19:18).

Consider an issue you've been puzzling over, a decision you need to make, or an approach you need to take with a difficult person. How does Jesus' simple but majestic summary help you?

PRAY

Ask God to help you love him "with all your passion and prayer and intelligence and energy." Take one at a time, if you wish. Then consider someone you know. Ask God to help you love that person the way you already love yourself. (You feed yourself, you clothe yourself, you give yourself a place to live — that's love.)

LIVE

Picture Jesus saying to you, "Love the Lord God with all your passion and prayer and intelligence and energy. . . . Love others as well as you love yourself." Don't take this as a scolding but as the best, wisest thing any person could do.

18

PETER BLOWS IT

MARK 14:66-72

66-67   While all this was going on, Peter was down in the courtyard. One of the Chief Priest's servant girls came in and, seeing Peter warming himself there, looked hard at him and said, "You were with the Nazarene, Jesus."

68   He denied it: "I don't know what you're talking about." He went out on the porch. A rooster crowed.

69-70   The girl spotted him and began telling the people standing around, "He's one of them." He denied it again.

After a little while, the bystanders brought it up again. "You've *got* to be one of them. You've got 'Galilean' written all over you."

71-72   Now Peter got really nervous and swore, "I never laid eyes on this man you're talking about." Just then the rooster crowed a second time. Peter remembered how Jesus had said, "Before a rooster crows twice, you'll deny me three times." He collapsed in tears.

READ

As you read the passage, put yourself in Peter's sandals. To get a more vivid picture of what is happening, skim the expanded reading.

THINK

How does Peter feel to be in the courtyard? What has happened since his bold declaration of devotion to Jesus no matter what, earlier in the chapter? What thoughts shoot through Peter's mind that lead him to leave the fireside for the porch?

Now imagine that the rooster has crowed and reality is caving in on Peter. Sit beside him in his anguish. What is he experiencing? As he remembers Jesus' words, what does Jesus' face look like in his mind's eye? What are the tones of Jesus' voice?

PRAY/LIVE

Let your meditation on Peter's failure lead you to consider your own heart and life. Where have you blown it lately? Talk to Jesus about this. Bravely let yourself feel the depth of what you've done. You might speak a prayer of humility or thanksgiving, or a request for something you need. Notice what you expect Jesus to do or say in response.

Now read the passage again slowly. What is Jesus saying in response to you? Be open to how he may be reacting differently to you or to your failure than you expected. Write down what Jesus' response was and what experiencing that was like.

THE MAIN CHARACTER IN THIS DRAMA

LUKE 3:16-20

16-17 But John intervened: "I'm baptizing you here in the river. The main character in this drama, to whom I'm a mere stagehand, will ignite the kingdom life, a fire, the Holy Spirit within you, changing you from the inside out. He's going to clean house — make a clean sweep of your lives. He'll place everything true in its proper place before God; everything false he'll put out with the trash to be burned."

18-20 There was a lot more of this — words that gave strength to the people, words that put heart in them. The Message! But Herod, the ruler, stung by John's rebuke in the matter of Herodias, his brother Philip's wife, capped his long string of evil deeds with this outrage: He put John in jail.

READ

Read the passage aloud four times, each time reading it with a different volume.

THINK

These verses tell us about John the Baptist, a torchbearer for the coming of Jesus' ministry, calling people to repent.

Focus first on the words describing "the main character in this drama." In your life, what would it mean to be a "mere stagehand" where the main character is Jesus? What might be some areas of your life where the Holy Spirit will make a clean sweep, changing you?

Now think about John's responses in the first few verses of the passage, concerning generosity, justice, and honesty.

PRAY

What do you need to repent of in areas where you have failed to be generous, just, and honest in the past week? Invite the Holy Spirit to put everything false "out with the trash to be burned."

Ask God to help you grow in generosity — for example, with your money, time, gifts, passions, energy, and so on.

Ask God to help you grow as an advocate for justice — for example, in your neighborhood, in your city, for the poor, for the unborn, for other people in the world, and so on.

Ask God to reveal areas of dishonesty or deception in your life. Implore him to give you the grace and courage to live a life of honesty and integrity.

LIVE

Live generously, justly, and honestly today, as a mere stagehand to the main character in this drama: Jesus.

DAY 21

GOD ENCOUNTERS

On this seventh day, review and reflect on all you have read this week. Take the time to revel in the ways you've encountered God in the past six days.

NO RUN-OF-THE-MILL SINNER

LUKE 6:27-36

27-30 "To you who are ready for the truth, I say this: Love your enemies. Let them bring out the best in you, not the worst. When someone gives you a hard time, respond with the energies of prayer for that person. If someone slaps you in the face, stand there and take it. If someone grabs your shirt, giftwrap your best coat and make a present of it. If someone takes unfair advantage of you, use the occasion to practice the servant life. No more tit-for-tat stuff. Live generously.

31-34 "Here is a simple rule of thumb for behavior: Ask yourself what you want people to do for you; then grab the initiative and do it for *them*! If you only love the lovable, do you expect a pat on the back? Run-of-the-mill sinners do that. If you only help those who help you, do you expect a medal? Garden-variety sinners do that. If you only give for what you hope to get out of it, do you think that's charity? The stingiest of pawnbrokers does that.

35-36 "I tell you, love your enemies. Help and give without expecting a return. You'll never — I promise — regret it. Live out this God-created identity the way our Father lives toward us, generously and graciously, even when we're at our worst. Our Father is kind; you be kind."

READ
Read the passage aloud slowly.

THINK
Read the passage aloud a second time, but pretend you are Jesus. Get into it and read it like you mean it; say the words and phrases the way you think he would have. Perhaps gently? Perhaps warmly? Perhaps passionately?

Read the passage aloud one more time, but this time put yourself in the place of Jesus' listener; you're sitting in the front row as Jesus speaks and looks directly at you.

1. If Jesus spoke these words to you, what would they mean?
2. Which words would stand out to you?
3. What might Jesus be trying to get across to you?

PRAY
Thank our kind God that he loves his enemies. Thank God that he loves you when you act as if you barely know him. Take the words that stood out to you (see question 2) and paraphrase those back to God in prayer.

LIVE
Sit quietly and picture the kind of person you would be if you were to:

- let your enemies "bring out the best in you"
- respond with the energies of prayer for people
- "practice the servant life" when someone is unfair
- "live generously"
- give without expecting in return

DO YOU SEE THIS WOMAN?

LUKE 7:37-47

37-39 Just then a woman of the village, the town harlot, having learned that Jesus was a guest in the home of the Pharisee, came with a bottle of very expensive perfume and stood at his feet, weeping, raining tears on his feet. Letting down her hair, she dried his feet, kissed them, and anointed them with the perfume. When the Pharisee who had invited him saw this, he said to himself, "If this man was the prophet I thought he was, he would have known what kind of woman this is who is falling all over him."

40 Jesus said to him, "Simon, I have something to tell you."

"Oh? Tell me."

41-42 "Two men were in debt to a banker. One owed five hundred silver pieces, the other fifty. Neither of them could pay up, and so the banker canceled both debts. Which of the two would be more grateful?"

43-47 Simon answered, "I suppose the one who was forgiven the most."

"That's right," said Jesus. Then turning to the woman, but speaking to Simon, he said, "Do you see this woman? I came to your home; you provided no water for my feet, but she rained tears on my feet and dried them with her hair. You gave me no greeting, but from the time I arrived she hasn't quit kissing my feet. You provided nothing for freshening up, but she has soothed my feet with perfume. Impressive, isn't it? She was forgiven many, many sins, and so she is very, very grateful. If the forgiveness is minimal, the gratitude is minimal."

READ

Read the passage slowly, noticing the major players and actions in the story. Picture the setting's sounds, smells, and sights.

THINK

Now choose one person in the story with whom you identify most — the Pharisee, the town harlot, or an onlooker — and read the story again. Imaginatively enter the scene, experiencing everything from that person's perspective. Hear the conversations. Feel the silence in the room as Jesus' feet are tenderly washed. Now listen to Jesus' voice and watch his face as he speaks. What do you feel? What thoughts go through your head?

PRAY

Talk with Jesus about what this experience has stirred up in you.

LIVE

Oswald Chambers said, "If human love does not carry a man beyond himself, it is not love. If love is always discreet, always wise, always sensible and calculating, never carried beyond itself, it is not love at all. It may be affection, it may be warmth of feeling, but it has not the true nature of love in it."[3]

Think about the degree of restraint or abandon you show in your relationship with Jesus (and with others). Consider the conscious or unconscious decisions you are constantly making about the way you'll act in that relationship. When does emotional momentum stir you? What do you do when it does? Under what circumstances do you set limits or hold back? What expectations or fears underlie your decisions? Share these with Jesus. What is something you could do today that would have "the true nature of love in it"?

SITTING BEFORE THE MASTER

LUKE 10:38-42

38-40   As they continued their travel, Jesus entered a village. A woman by the name of Martha welcomed him and made him feel quite at home. She had a sister, Mary, who sat before the Master, hanging on every word he said. But Martha was pulled away by all she had to do in the kitchen. Later, she stepped in, interrupting them. "Master, don't you care that my sister has abandoned the kitchen to me? Tell her to lend me a hand."

41-42   The Master said, "Martha, dear Martha, you're fussing far too much and getting yourself worked up over nothing. One thing only is essential, and Mary has chosen it — it's the main course, and won't be taken from her."

READ

This passage might be very familiar to you. So before reading, pause and ask God to give you fresh eyes and an open heart to absorb it. Then read it carefully.

THINK

Prayerfully let your creativity loose as you engage with this text. First put yourself in the skin of Mary. On that day, what might you be doing? What's going on around you in the house? What are you thinking and feeling when Martha complains about you?

Now, put yourself in Martha's shoes. What are you preparing? What are your motivations? What are you feeling? What might you be thinking and feeling after Jesus says those words to you?

LIVE

The text says that Mary "sat before the Master." Now it's your turn. Take an empty chair and place it in the middle of the room. Sit or kneel in front of it, imagining Jesus seated there. Read the passage again. Stay in this posture, in the silence, and ponder who Jesus is.

PRAY

As you remain before the chair, whisper, "Jesus, who am I more like today: Mary or Martha?" Don't rush this experience. Even if an urge to get up comes, continue to be still and sit in silence. Anticipate that Jesus will communicate with you. Wait for him and allow him to speak words of promise, correction, or comfort into your life.

LIVING IN GOD-REALITY

LUKE 12:25-34

25-28 "Has anyone by fussing before the mirror ever gotten taller by so much as an inch? If fussing can't even do that, why fuss at all? Walk into the fields and look at the wildflowers. They don't fuss with their appearance — but have you ever seen color and design quite like it? The ten best-dressed men and women in the country look shabby alongside them. If God gives such attention to the wildflowers, most of them never even seen, don't you think he'll attend to you, take pride in you, do his best for you?

29-32 "What I'm trying to do here is get you to relax, not be so preoccupied with *getting* so you can respond to God's *giving*. People who don't know God and the way he works fuss over these things, but you know both God and how he works. Steep yourself in God-reality, God-initiative, God-provisions. You'll find all your everyday human concerns will be met. Don't be afraid of missing out. You're my dearest friends! The Father wants to give you the very kingdom itself.

33-34 "Be generous. Give to the poor. Get yourselves a bank that can't go bankrupt, a bank in heaven far from bankrobbers, safe from embezzlers, a bank you can bank on. It's obvious, isn't it? The place where your treasure is, is the place you will most want to be, and end up being."

READ

Read the passage aloud slowly. Pretend you and Jesus are sitting in Starbucks, and he's saying these words to you quietly.

THINK

Now pretend that you've come home, and you're going over in your mind what Jesus said to you. Read the passage again.

1. What words or phrases draw you the most?
2. What do you think Jesus is trying to say to you?
3. In order to do what Jesus said, what are you going to have to really trust for?

   ☐ that he'll "do his best for you"
   ☐ that by *giving* instead of *getting,* you'll still have everything you need
   ☐ that "God-reality, God-initiative, God-provisions" are really enough
   ☐ other:

4. How do you feel about this?

PRAY

Respond to God about truly trusting him for these practical, important matters. Be honest about what you are — and are not — ready to do.

LIVE

Sit quietly before God. Receive from him the idea that he is your treasure: "The place where your treasure is, is the place you will most want to be, and end up being."

LOST AND FOUND

LUKE 15:1-10

1-3   By this time a lot of men and women of doubtful reputation were hanging around Jesus, listening intently. The Pharisees and religion scholars were not pleased, not at all pleased. They growled, "He takes in sinners and eats meals with them, treating them like old friends." Their grumbling triggered this story.

4-7   "Suppose one of you had a hundred sheep and lost one. Wouldn't you leave the ninety-nine in the wilderness and go after the lost one until you found it? When found, you can be sure you would put it across your shoulders, rejoicing, and when you got home call in your friends and neighbors, saying, 'Celebrate with me! I've found my lost sheep!' Count on it — there's more joy in heaven over one sinner's rescued life than over ninety-nine good people in no need of rescue.

8-10   "Or imagine a woman who has ten coins and loses one. Won't she light a lamp and scour the house, looking in every nook and cranny until she finds it? And when she finds it you can be sure she'll call her friends and neighbors: 'Celebrate with me! I found my lost coin!' Count on it — that's the kind of party God's angels throw every time one lost soul turns to God."

READ

Open your hands with your palms facing up. Sit for a moment in stillness and ask your heavenly Father to tell you important words that you need to hear today. Communicate that you are open to his guidance. Now read the passage.

THINK

In this passage two things — a sheep and a coin — are lost and then found. And both are celebrated upon their return.

As you think about the two stories of the lost items, which story hits you the most right now? Contemplate why that story jumps out at you today. Read it again, and put yourself in it.

When have you felt lost? Why did you feel that way?

In both stories people — a shepherd, a woman — proactively went after the lost item. How does it feel to know that God himself is proactively pursuing you for the simple yet profound fact that he loves you deeply?

Notice the element of celebration in these stories. What does this celebration make you feel? What should you begin to celebrate in your life or in the lives of others?

PRAY

Listen for God in these areas: What might he be communicating to you regarding your lostness? Regarding the fact that he desires to find you? Regarding how he celebrates your life?

LIVE

Recognize what God is doing in the world today — in the spectacular and in the mundane — and then celebrate it.

RETURNING TO SAY THANK YOU

LUKE 17:11-19

11-13   It happened that as he made his way toward Jerusalem, he crossed over the border between Samaria and Galilee. As he entered a village, ten men, all lepers, met him. They kept their distance but raised their voices, calling out, "Jesus, Master, have mercy on us!"

14-16   Taking a good look at them, he said, "Go, show yourselves to the priests."

They went, and while still on their way, became clean. One of them, when he realized that he was healed, turned around and came back, shouting his gratitude, glorifying God. He kneeled at Jesus' feet, so grateful. He couldn't thank him enough — and he was a Samaritan.

17-19   Jesus said, "Were not ten healed? Where are the nine? Can none be found to come back and give glory to God except this outsider?" Then he said to him, "Get up. On your way. Your faith has healed and saved you."

READ

Read the passage, focusing especially on the questions Jesus asks.

THINK

Not only are lepers deformed by their disease, but Old Testament law also excludes them from community with others. Ten men come to Jesus with this horrific skin disease. These men are physical and relational outsiders. When Jesus heals them, he also helps restore them to their communities.

When have you felt like an outsider and then experienced God's restoring you to community with others or with himself? Do you tend to be like the nine, who asked for God's help and didn't return, or are you like the one who returned to say thank you? Why?

Think about your last several requests to God in prayer. Have you turned around and come back, shouting your gratitude for how he has answered your requests and blessed you in the process? Why or why not? What needs to happen in your life for you to remember to return when God answers your prayers?

PRAY

Make this prayer time one of intentional thankfulness. Consider your recent requests to God (being specific). Return now and thank him for answering those requests, big and small.

LIVE

Every time you make a request, turn around and shout your gratitude.

DAY 28

GOD ENCOUNTERS

On this seventh day, review and reflect on all you have read this week. Take the time to revel in the ways you've encountered God in the past six days.

HEALING THE ENEMY

LUKE 22:47-53

47-48   No sooner were the words out of his mouth than a crowd showed up, Judas, the one from the Twelve, in the lead. He came right up to Jesus to kiss him. Jesus said, "Judas, you would betray the Son of Man with a kiss?"

49-50   When those with him saw what was happening, they said, "Master, shall we fight?" One of them took a swing at the Chief Priest's servant and cut off his right ear.

51   Jesus said, "Let them be. Even in this." Then, touching the servant's ear, he healed him.

52-53   Jesus spoke to those who had come — high priests, Temple police, religion leaders: "What is this, jumping me with swords and clubs as if I were a dangerous criminal? Day after day I've been with you in the Temple and you've not so much as lifted a hand against me. But do it your way — it's a dark night, a dark hour."

READ

Read the passage aloud slowly. Keep in mind that this occurs in the Garden of Gethsemane. Jesus has just prayed, "Father, remove this cup from me. But please, not what I want. What do *you* want?" Then Jesus noted that his disciples were sleeping when he'd asked them to watch with him (see verses 42-46).

THINK

Read the passage again. This time place yourself in the scene as one of the disciples watching what is going on.

1. How do you feel when Judas arrives with soldiers?
2. How do you feel when one of you strikes the chief priest's servant?
3. How do you feel when Jesus heals this servant — one of his attackers?
4. How do you feel when Jesus points out how silly and dramatic his assailants are? (He has been accessible to them for days and is now *letting them* arrest him.)

Finally, put yourself in the place of the servant of the chief priest who is healed by Jesus. How do you feel? What do you want to say to Jesus?

PRAY

Consider Jesus' behavior in this scene. What baffles you? What is awakened within you? Fear? A sense of worship? If there is any way this scene might help you trust Jesus more, tell him.

LIVE

Sit quietly with your hand on one of your ears. See yourself as someone who is about to injure Jesus, but instead he heals you from your own injuries. Sit in that sense of being healed by God. Sit in that sense of finally being able to hear Jesus in your heart with your willing ears.

LOOKING FOR THE LIVING ONE IN A CEMETERY

LUKE 24:1-12

1-3   At the crack of dawn on Sunday, the women came to the tomb carrying the burial spices they had prepared. They found the entrance stone rolled back from the tomb, so they walked in. But once inside, they couldn't find the body of the Master Jesus.

4-8   They were puzzled, wondering what to make of this. Then, out of nowhere it seemed, two men, light cascading over them, stood there. The women were awestruck and bowed down in worship. The men said, "Why are you looking for the Living One in a cemetery? He is not here, but raised up. Remember how he told you when you were still back in Galilee that he had to be handed over to sinners, be killed on a cross, and in three days rise up?" Then they remembered Jesus' words.

9-11   They left the tomb and broke the news of all this to the Eleven and the rest. Mary Magdalene, Joanna, Mary the mother of James, and the other women with them kept telling these things to the apostles, but the apostles didn't believe a word of it, thought they were making it all up.

12   But Peter jumped to his feet and ran to the tomb. He stooped to look in and saw a few grave clothes, that's all. He walked away puzzled, shaking his head.

READ

Read the passage carefully, paying attention to the various characters and their responses to the events of the story.

THINK

Which disciple or follower of Jesus do you most identify with in this passage? What is it about that person that reminds you of yourself?

Read the passage again, this time putting yourself in that person's position. What are your thoughts and feelings as you hear that Jesus is alive again? What runs through your mind as you see others' responses? What do you wonder about? Where do you go when you hear the news? What questions do you have?

PRAY

Now picture the risen Jesus approaching you later that day, inviting you to spend time with him. How do you interact with him? What do you say? Talk to him about what all of this has been like for you.

LIVE

Reflect on your prayer time. You might again consider the person in the story you chose and why, or you could think about how your understanding of faithfulness and discipleship was deepened or changed. Write down anything that seems significant.

LIFE-LIGHT

JOHN 1:12-18

12-13   But whoever did want him,
            who believed he was who he claimed
            and would do what he said,
        He made to be their true selves,
            their child-of-God selves.
        These are the God-begotten,
            not blood-begotten,
            not flesh-begotten,
            not sex-begotten.

14   The Word became flesh and blood,
            and moved into the neighborhood.
        We saw the glory with our own eyes,
            the one-of-a-kind glory,
            like Father, like Son,
        Generous inside and out,
            true from start to finish.

15   John pointed him out and called, "This is the One! The One I told you
        was coming after me but in fact was ahead of me. He has always been
        ahead of me, has always had the first word."

16-18   We all live off his generous bounty,
            gift after gift after gift.
        We got the basics from Moses,
            and then this exuberant giving and receiving,
        This endless knowing and understanding—
            all this came through Jesus, the Messiah.
        No one has ever seen God,
            not so much as a glimpse.
        This one-of-a-kind God-Expression,
            who exists at the very heart of the Father,
            has made him plain as day.

READ

Read the passage slowly and repeatedly. Don't rush through it. Take your time. Ruminate on the passage. Let it sink into the well of your soul.

THINK

What sticks out to you the most in these verses? Why is the Word coming to Earth such a big deal in the great scope of human history?

"The Word became flesh and blood, and moved into the neighborhood." What might your life be like if God moved into the house or apartment or locker or dorm room next to yours?

How might the environment of your neighborhood be different if he were your next-door neighbor? How might your own life be different? Be specific.

LIVE

Get a candle (if you don't have one, buy or borrow one). At night, go into a dark room (turn off any lights and shut any curtains). Light the candle and stare at the flame. Consider Jesus, the Word, coming to Earth in flesh and blood, becoming the Life-Light for the world.

PRAY

Stand in the dark room, still looking at the small flame. Allow these words to guide your prayers: "What came into existence was Life, and the Life was Light to live by. The Life-Light blazed out of darkness; the darkness couldn't put it out" (John 1:4-5).

TRUSTING AND EXPECTANT

JOHN 3:9-11,14-15,17-21

9-11 Nicodemus asked, "What do you mean by this? How does this happen?"

Jesus said, "You're a respected teacher of Israel and you don't know these basics? Listen carefully. I'm speaking sober truth to you. I speak only of what I know by experience; I give witness only to what I have seen with my own eyes. There is nothing secondhand here, no hearsay. Yet instead of facing the evidence and accepting it, you procrastinate with questions." . . .

14-15 "In the same way that Moses lifted the serpent in the desert so people could have something to see and then believe, it is necessary for the Son of Man to be lifted up — and everyone who looks up to him, trusting and expectant, will gain a real life, eternal life. . . .

17-18 "God didn't go to all the trouble of sending his Son merely to point an accusing finger, telling the world how bad it was. He came to help, to put the world right again. Anyone who trusts in him is acquitted; anyone who refuses to trust him has long since been under the death sentence without knowing it. And why? Because of that person's failure to believe in the one-of-a-kind Son of God when introduced to him.

19-21 "This is the crisis we're in: God-light streamed into the world, but men and women everywhere ran for the darkness. They went for the darkness because they were not really interested in pleasing God. Everyone who makes a practice of doing evil, addicted to denial and illusion, hates God-light and won't come near it, fearing a painful exposure. But anyone working and living in truth and reality welcomes God-light so the work can be seen for the God-work it is."

READ

Before you read the passage, understand that Jesus has just told Nicodemus (a scholar and teacher) that he must be "'born from above' by the wind of God, the Spirit of God" (verse 8). But Nicodemus is confused! Now read the passage silently.

THINK

Read the passage again, aloud this time, putting yourself in the place of Nicodemus standing on the rooftop in the moonlight, receiving Jesus' words.

1. Which words or phrases stand out to you? Consider these:

   ☐ "Everyone who looks up to him, trusting and expectant, will gain a real life, eternal life."
   ☐ "God didn't go to all the trouble of sending his Son merely to point an accusing finger, . . . [the Son] came to help, to put the world right again."
   ☐ "Anyone who trusts in him is acquitted."
   ☐ "God-light streamed into the world."
   ☐ "Anyone working and living in truth and reality welcomes God-light so the work can be seen for the God-work it is."

2. Why?

PRAY

Talk to Jesus about any phrases that confused you. Talk to him about the phrases that captivated you.

LIVE

Sit quietly before God. Put yourself in the place of Nicodemus again — possibly lying in your bed each night, going over these words Jesus said to you. Which words will you drift off with tonight?

DO YOU WANT TO GET WELL?

JOHN 5:1-9

1-6   Soon another Feast came around and Jesus was back in Jerusalem. Near the Sheep Gate in Jerusalem there was a pool, in Hebrew called *Bethesda*, with five alcoves. Hundreds of sick people — blind, crippled, paralyzed — were in these alcoves. One man had been an invalid there for thirty-eight years. When Jesus saw him stretched out by the pool and knew how long he had been there, he said, "Do you want to get well?"

7   The sick man said, "Sir, when the water is stirred, I don't have anybody to put me in the pool. By the time I get there, somebody else is already in."

8-9   Jesus said, "Get up, take your bedroll, start walking." The man was healed on the spot. He picked up his bedroll and walked off.

That day happened to be the Sabbath.

READ

Read this passage, being especially aware of how it depicts sickness, lack of wholeness, and the process of healing. These details might remind you of a truth you've considered before, or they might reveal something altogether new.

THINK

Read the verses again. What stands out to you? Why might the Holy Spirit be bringing this to your attention? Perhaps you deeply desire to experience wholeness of mind or spirit because you have been experiencing your woundedness lately. Or perhaps you find yourself questioning whether Jesus really can heal a physical sickness — either your own or someone else's.

PRAY

Ask Jesus what he has specifically for you that calls for healing. Talk to him about what you hear.

These possibilities might help get you started: Allowing Jesus to bring healing might require you to let go of something that hurts too much to release, and you don't think you're ready for it right now. Or you desire freedom and wholeness, but you feel stuck, imprisoned, fragmented. Or in this moment you find yourself ready for your healing: Be open to the possibility of Jesus bringing healing when you least expect it, of being "healed on the spot." On the other hand, perhaps you feel ready and are frustrated that nothing seems to be happening.

LIVE

If your time with Jesus and God's Message today moved you the tiniest bit closer to wholeness, rejoice. If not, simply let things be. Continue talking to Jesus about your situation, being alert to what he has for you.

NO CONDEMNATION

JOHN 8:1-11

1-2   Jesus went across to Mount Olives, but he was soon back in the Temple again. Swarms of people came to him. He sat down and taught them.

3-6   The religion scholars and Pharisees led in a woman who had been caught in an act of adultery. They stood her in plain sight of everyone and said, "Teacher, this woman was caught red-handed in the act of adultery. Moses, in the Law, gives orders to stone such persons. What do you say?" They were trying to trap him into saying something incriminating so they could bring charges against him.

6-8   Jesus bent down and wrote with his finger in the dirt. They kept at him, badgering him. He straightened up and said, "The sinless one among you, go first: Throw the stone." Bending down again, he wrote some more in the dirt.

9-10 Hearing that, they walked away, one after another, beginning with the oldest. The woman was left alone. Jesus stood up and spoke to her. "Woman, where are they? Does no one condemn you?"

11   "No one, Master."

"Neither do I," said Jesus. "Go on your way. From now on, don't sin."

READ

Write out today's passage. Say each word aloud as you go.

THINK

Imagine yourself in the crowd the day these events unfold. Picture the embarrassed and shamed expression on the woman's face. Hear the condescending voices of the religious leaders. Feel the Middle Eastern dirt blowing against you as Jesus bends down and writes something in it.

Now imagine yourself in the same situation as this woman. You're caught in a horrendous sin, exposed. Imagine you and Jesus having the same conversation:

"Does no one condemn you?"

"No one, Master."

He looks you in the eyes. "Neither do I. Go on your way. From now on don't sin."

What are you feeling? Thinking?

PRAY

Confess those acts of spiritual adultery you've engaged in recently. Close your eyes and imagine Jesus standing before you. Hear him telling you that he doesn't condemn you but that he wants you to stop sinning from now on.

LIVE

Ask the Holy Spirit to give you wisdom and guidance not to condone other people's (or your own) sin and at the same time not to condemn those people (or yourself) either. Ask the Spirit to bring to your mind people you can love while avoiding condemning and condoning.

DAY 35

GOD ENCOUNTERS

On this seventh day, review and reflect on all you have read this week. Take the time to revel in the ways you've encountered God in the past six days.

KNOWING THE GOOD SHEPHERD

JOHN 10:2-5,14-18

2-5   "The shepherd walks right up to the gate. The gatekeeper opens the gate to him and the sheep recognize his voice. He calls his own sheep by name and leads them out. When he gets them all out, he leads them and they follow because they are familiar with his voice. They won't follow a stranger's voice but will scatter because they aren't used to the sound of it." . . .

14-18   "I am the Good Shepherd. I know my own sheep and my own sheep know me. In the same way, the Father knows me and I know the Father. I put the sheep before myself, sacrificing myself if necessary. You need to know that I have other sheep in addition to those in this pen. I need to gather and bring them, too. They'll also recognize my voice. Then it will be one flock, one Shepherd. This is why the Father loves me: because I freely lay down my life. And so I am free to take it up again. No one takes it from me. I lay it down of my own free will. I have the right to lay it down; I also have the right to take it up again. I received this authority personally from my Father."

READ

Read these words of Jesus aloud slowly. Notice the two sets of closeness expressed: between Jesus and the Father, and between Jesus and the sheep.

THINK

Read these words of Jesus again aloud, as if he were explaining this to you personally. Notice that the word *know* occurs five times. Jesus knows his sheep; they know Jesus. The Father knows Jesus; Jesus knows the Father.

1. What do you make of the centrality of knowing one another?
2. Jesus, the Good Shepherd, does the following for the sheep. Which of these do you most need for Jesus to do for you today?

   ☐ call his own sheep by name
   ☐ lead them out
   ☐ know his own sheep
   ☐ put the sheep before himself, sacrificing himself, if necessary
   ☐ gather and bring other sheep

3. The sheep recognize Jesus' voice and respond by following him and knowing him. How do you need to respond to Jesus today?
4. How are you growing in your capacity to recognize his voice, perhaps through your experiences in this book?

PRAY

Talk to Jesus about what you need from him. Especially talk about your capacity to recognize his voice. Ask for help with this.

LIVE

Sit quietly before God and practice alert waiting. Receive the assurance that such practice will help you be more alert to Jesus' voice when you hear it.

HOLDING ON TO LIFE

JOHN 12:20-26

20-21   There were some Greeks in town who had come up to worship at the Feast. They approached Philip, who was from Bethsaida in Galilee: "Sir, we want to see Jesus. Can you help us?"

22-23   Philip went and told Andrew. Andrew and Philip together told Jesus. Jesus answered, "Time's up. The time has come for the Son of Man to be glorified.

24-25   "Listen carefully: Unless a grain of wheat is buried in the ground, dead to the world, it is never any more than a grain of wheat. But if it is buried, it sprouts and reproduces itself many times over. In the same way, anyone who holds on to life just as it is destroys that life. But if you let it go, reckless in your love, you'll have it forever, real and eternal.

26   "If any of you wants to serve me, then follow me. Then you'll be where I am, ready to serve at a moment's notice. The Father will honor and reward anyone who serves me."

BEAR

If possible, read the expanded passage to see the full picture of what is happening here. Then read this excerpt three times meditatively.

THINK

Write in your own words what you think Jesus means when he talks about a grain of wheat dying and reproducing itself. Think about what you wrote.

Now wait for Jesus to show you an area of your life — a relationship, a decision to be made, and so on — in which you are "hold[ing] on to life just as it is," and not allowing him to bring growth or change. In what ways might your stance be destructive or suffocating?

Ponder Romans 12:2: "Fix your attention on God. You'll be changed from the inside out." What would this area of your life look like if you were to "fix your attention on God," and in so doing, let go?

PRAY

Sit down. Hold your hands in tight fists. Then relax them, open them, and turn your palms upward. Talk with Jesus about what a life of open hands would look like. Ask him to show you what it means to "be where [he is]."

LIVE

Think again about your tightly held part of life. Try being "reckless in your love": let go just a little bit, with Jesus' help. Serve Jesus today. Follow him today.

THE FRIEND

JOHN 14:15-17

15-17   "If you love me, show it by doing what I've told you. I will talk to the Father, and he'll provide you another Friend so that you will always have someone with you. This Friend is the Spirit of Truth. The godless world can't take him in because it doesn't have eyes to see him, doesn't know what to look for. But you know him already because he has been staying with you, and will even be *in* you!"

READ

Because this passage is about the Holy Spirit, ask him to guide you in a prayerful reading of it. Make your reading a prayer in itself.

THINK

The Holy Spirit is the most neglected personhood of God. We often treat the Spirit like a tagalong part of the Trinity. Yet Jesus promises to leave his disciples (and us as his followers) with this important Friend. Is it hard for you to imagine that the Holy Spirit is offered to you as a friend? Why or why not?

What does it mean to have the Holy Spirit in you and guiding you throughout your day, as this passage says: "But you know him already because he has been staying with you, and will even be *in* you"? Is it comforting? Discomforting? Frustrating? Hard to comprehend? Awe-inspiring? How can you grow today in awareness that the Friend lives in you?

PRAY

Ask the Holy Spirit, your Friend, to remind you of his presence. Pray the words of this Scripture, asking him to "make everything plain to you" (verse 26) and reminding you of all the things that Jesus told the disciples (and you).

LIVE

As you drive, walk, work, study, and interact with others today, call on your Friend for his guidance with the thoughts you think, the words you speak, and the decisions you make.

ONE HEART AND MIND

JOHN 17:20-23,26

20-23
I'm praying not only for them
But also for those who will believe in me
Because of them and their witness about me.
The goal is for all of them to become one heart and mind —
Just as you, Father, are in me and I in you,
So they might be one heart and mind with us.
Then the world might believe that you, in fact, sent me.
The same glory you gave me, I gave them,
So they'll be as unified and together as we are —
I in them and you in me.
Then they'll be mature in this oneness,
And give the godless world evidence
That you've sent me and loved them
In the same way you've loved me.

. . . .

26
I have made your very being known to them —
Who you are and what you do —
And continue to make it known,
So that your love for me
Might be in them
Exactly as I am in them.

READ

Read the passage aloud slowly, remembering that this is Jesus praying for you ("those who will believe in me").

THINK

Read it again slowly, but this time substitute your name (or your name and "all of them") when you read *them* or *they*.

If you need to, read the passage one more time before considering these questions.

1. What are you most excited about Jesus praying for you or saying about you?

   ☐ your witness for Jesus
   ☐ to be one heart and mind with other followers of Jesus
   ☐ to be one heart and mind with God and Jesus
   ☐ that Jesus has given you glory
   ☐ that Jesus is in you
   ☐ that you'll be mature in oneness
   ☐ that you'll give the world evidence that God sent Jesus
   ☐ that Jesus made the very being of God known to you
   ☐ that God's love for Jesus is in you
   ☐ that Jesus is in you

2. Why?

PRAY

Thank Jesus for praying for you. Talk to him about the prayer phrases you found most meaningful. Pray Jesus' prayer for his followers alive today in the world.

LIVE

Walk around today with the sense that Jesus is in you and that this was always his plan — to be in you.

TAKE YOUR FINGER AND EXAMINE MY HANDS

JOHN 20:19-29

19-20 Later on that day, the disciples had gathered together, but, fearful of the Jews, had locked all the doors in the house. Jesus entered, stood among them, and said, "Peace to you." Then he showed them his hands and side.

20-21 The disciples, seeing the Master with their own eyes, were exuberant. Jesus repeated his greeting: "Peace to you. Just as the Father sent me, I send you."

22-23 Then he took a deep breath and breathed into them. "Receive the Holy Spirit," he said. "If you forgive someone's sins, they're gone for good. If you don't forgive sins, what are you going to do with them?"

24-25 But Thomas, sometimes called the Twin, one of the Twelve, was not with them when Jesus came. The other disciples told him, "We saw the Master."

But he said, "Unless I see the nail holes in his hands, put my finger in the nail holes, and stick my hand in his side, I won't believe it."

26 Eight days later, his disciples were again in the room. This time Thomas was with them. Jesus came through the locked doors, stood among them, and said, "Peace to you."

27 Then he focused his attention on Thomas. "Take your finger and examine my hands. Take your hand and stick it in my side. Don't be unbelieving. Believe."

28 Thomas said, "My Master! My God!"

29 Jesus said, "So, you believe because you've seen with your own eyes. Even better blessings are in store for those who believe without seeing."

READ

Read John's description of the first time Jesus appeared to his disciples after his death and resurrection. Pay special attention to Jesus' words to them.

THINK

What does Thomas's response to Jesus' resurrection make you feel? How do you react to Thomas's disbelief? What about Jesus' response to him?

PRAY

Read the passage once more. This time pretend you are one of the disciples. Maybe you will be a believing disciple; maybe you will be Thomas. Pick a role that corresponds with where you actually are in your relationship with Jesus right now. Now play out the story. As you hear Jesus speak to you, respond to him from your heart. Let him engage you in conversation.

LIVE

If you're a Thomas, wonder what it would be like to "believe without seeing." If you're like the other disciples, remember to offer grace to others who need to see before believing. Thank God for the faith he has given you — either way.

GOD'S REDEMPTIVE PLAN

ACTS 1:1-11

1-5   Dear Theophilus, in the first volume of this book I wrote on everything that Jesus began to do and teach until the day he said good-bye to the apostles, the ones he had chosen through the Holy Spirit, and was taken up to heaven. After his death, he presented himself alive to them in many different settings over a period of forty days. In face-to-face meetings, he talked to them about things concerning the kingdom of God. As they met and ate meals together, he told them that they were on no account to leave Jerusalem but "must wait for what the Father promised: the promise you heard from me. John baptized in water; you will be baptized in the Holy Spirit. And soon."

6   When they were together for the last time they asked, "Master, are you going to restore the kingdom to Israel now? Is this the time?"

7-8   He told them, "You don't get to know the time. Timing is the Father's business. What you'll get is the Holy Spirit. And when the Holy Spirit comes on you, you will be able to be my witnesses in Jerusalem, all over Judea and Samaria, even to the ends of the world."

9-11   These were his last words. As they watched, he was taken up and disappeared in a cloud. They stood there, staring into the empty sky. Suddenly two men appeared — in white robes! They said, "You Galileans! — why do you just stand here looking up at an empty sky? This very Jesus who was taken up from among you to heaven will come as certainly — and mysteriously — as he left."

READ

Read the passage from the perspective of someone who has never read it before.

THINK

When are you tempted to be a spectator to the movements of God's redemptive plan rather than a participant involved in the action? Why? What are specific ways you can get off the bench and get up to bat for what God is up to in the world? What are some ways you can be a witness to others in your circle of influence?

You know that Jesus will come again in the future. What implications does that reality have on your life?

PRAY

Ask God to give you the courage to take the risk and get into the game, to participate in God's redemptive plan.

LIVE

Ask a close friend or family member to help pray, brainstorm, and discern the ways you can be a participant in God's redemptive plan for your life and the lives of those around you. Ask this person to keep you in check, reminding you that God wants his followers to act on what Jesus said and did.

DAY 42

GOD ENCOUNTERS

On this seventh day, review and reflect on all you have read this week. Take the time to revel in the ways you've encountered God in the past six days.

DAY 43
EXPANDED PASSAGE: ACTS 4

FEARLESS CONFIDENCE

ACTS 4:24-31

24-26   Hearing the report, they lifted their voices in a wonderful harmony in prayer: "Strong God, you made heaven and earth and sea and everything in them. By the Holy Spirit you spoke through the mouth of your servant and our father, David:

> Why the big noise, nations?
> Why the mean plots, peoples?
> Earth's leaders push for position,
> Potentates meet for summit talks,
> The God-deniers, the Messiah-defiers!

27-28   "For in fact they did meet — Herod and Pontius Pilate with nations and peoples, even Israel itself! — met in this very city to plot against your holy Son Jesus, the One you made Messiah, to carry out the plans you long ago set in motion.

29-30   "And now they're at it again! Take care of their threats and give your servants fearless confidence in preaching your Message, as you stretch out your hand to us in healings and miracles and wonders done in the name of your holy servant Jesus."

31   While they were praying, the place where they were meeting trembled and shook. They were all filled with the Holy Spirit and continued to speak God's Word with fearless confidence.

READ

Read the passage aloud slowly, keeping in mind that Peter and John were just released from police custody for preaching about Jesus. Most of this passage is their prayer.

THINK

Read the passage aloud again. What touches you most? How do you explain the "fearless confidence" of these men who have just suffered for Jesus?

Read the passage one more time, noting when a member of the Trinity is mentioned: God, Jesus (and his designation, Messiah), the Holy Spirit. Clearly, Peter and John, as well as these followers of Jesus, were living in the reality of the Trinity—active and living among them! What might it look like to live your life today immersed in the reality and power of the Trinity?

PRAY

Paraphrase the prayer of Peter, John, and Jesus' followers (verses 24-30) as it fits your life today, including what God has done in the past (verses 24-28), what is happening today (verse 29), and how you wish for God to work today (verse 30).

LIVE

Remind yourself throughout the day that a follower of Jesus is immersed in the Trinitarian reality—really!

JESUS, THE MASTER

ACTS 7:51–8:1

51-53 "And you continue, so bullheaded! Calluses on your hearts, flaps on your ears! Deliberately ignoring the Holy Spirit, you're just like your ancestors. Was there ever a prophet who didn't get the same treatment? Your ancestors killed anyone who dared talk about the coming of the Just One. And you've kept up the family tradition — traitors and murderers, all of you. You had God's Law handed to you by angels — gift-wrapped! — and you squandered it!"

54-56 At that point they went wild, a rioting mob of catcalls and whistles and invective. But Stephen, full of the Holy Spirit, hardly noticed — he only had eyes for God, whom he saw in all his glory with Jesus standing at his side. He said, "Oh! I see heaven wide open and the Son of Man standing at God's side!"

57-58 Yelling and hissing, the mob drowned him out. Now in full stampede, they dragged him out of town and pelted him with rocks. The ringleaders took off their coats and asked a young man named Saul to watch them.

59-60 As the rocks rained down, Stephen prayed, "Master Jesus, take my life." Then he knelt down, praying loud enough for everyone to hear, "Master, don't blame them for this sin" — his last words. Then he died.

1 Saul was right there, congratulating the killers.

READ

Read the passage aloud once. Then read it again silently and slowly, paying careful attention to your response.

THINK

Stephen calls Jesus "Master," and his actions agree. Have you ever read or heard stories of other martyrs like Stephen, people who died for Jesus' sake? What do these stories make you feel?

PRAY

Become aware of Jesus inviting you to share with him your thoughts and feelings. Perhaps stories of martyrdom make you angry, grieved, or afraid. Maybe you find yourself pulling away from such stories. You might have questions. Maybe you want only to sit silently with Jesus. As you open your heart's reaction to him, let that become your prayer.

LIVE

Read the passage again, this time prayerfully. Look for clues to help you discern Jesus' response to Stephen's martyrdom, as well as Jesus' response to you. Write down anything you want to remember or think about later.

THE MIRACULOUS RELEASE

ACTS 12:7-15

7-9   Suddenly there was an angel at his side and light flooding the room. The angel shook Peter and got him up: "Hurry!" The handcuffs fell off his wrists. The angel said, "Get dressed. Put on your shoes." Peter did it. Then, "Grab your coat and let's get out of here." Peter followed him, but didn't believe it was really an angel — he thought he was dreaming.

10-11   Past the first guard and then the second, they came to the iron gate that led into the city. It swung open before them on its own, and they were out on the street, free as the breeze. At the first intersection the angel left him, going his own way. That's when Peter realized it was no dream. "I can't believe it — this really happened! The Master sent his angel and rescued me from Herod's vicious little production and the spectacle the Jewish mob was looking forward to."

12-14   Still shaking his head, amazed, he went to Mary's house, the Mary who was John Mark's mother. The house was packed with praying friends. When he knocked on the door to the courtyard, a young woman named Rhoda came to see who it was. But when she recognized his voice — Peter's voice! — she was so excited and eager to tell everyone Peter was there that she forgot to open the door and left him standing in the street.

15   But they wouldn't believe her, dismissing her, dismissing her report. "You're crazy," they said. She stuck by her story, insisting. They still wouldn't believe her and said, "It must be his angel."

READ

Imagine you are in a roomful of your friends, and they have asked you to read them a story. With this scenario in mind, read the passage.

THINK

Good stories grab hold of us and won't let go. This story is no exception. Scripture sometimes "messes" with us in appropriate ways. How does this passage mess with you and your understanding of God?

The people praying for Peter's release from prison didn't believe it when he was standing at the door. They thought Rhoda was crazy or it must be someone else or an angel of Peter (but not Peter himself). Is it hard to believe that the Holy Spirit is powerful enough to perform such sensational acts? Why or why not? If this were to happen today, would you be skeptical or cynical? Why or why not?

How often do you pray for God to work and, when he does, react with shock or disbelief? What does this reveal about the faith behind your prayers?

PRAY

What can you pray that God will do — and *wholeheartedly believe* that he will answer? Pray for that with bold confidence and hope, knowing that God is powerful and is listening to your prayer.

LIVE

Be keenly aware today of how the Holy Spirit is working — in the sensational, in the mundane, or in both.

LIVE AS YOU WERE MEANT TO LIVE

ACTS 16:25-34

25-26 Along about midnight, Paul and Silas were at prayer and singing a robust hymn to God. The other prisoners couldn't believe their ears. Then, without warning, a huge earthquake! The jailhouse tottered, every door flew open, all the prisoners were loose.

27-28 Startled from sleep, the jailer saw all the doors swinging loose on their hinges. Assuming that all the prisoners had escaped, he pulled out his sword and was about to do himself in, figuring he was as good as dead anyway, when Paul stopped him: "Don't do that! We're all still here! Nobody's run away!"

29-31 The jailer got a torch and ran inside. Badly shaken, he collapsed in front of Paul and Silas. He led them out of the jail and asked, "Sirs, what do I have to do to be saved, to really live?" They said, "Put your entire trust in the Master Jesus. Then you'll live as you were meant to live — and everyone in your house included!"

32-34 They went on to spell out in detail the story of the Master — the entire family got in on this part. They never did get to bed that night. The jailer made them feel at home, dressed their wounds, and then — he couldn't wait till morning! — was baptized, he and everyone in his family. There in his home, he had food set out for a festive meal. It was a night to remember: He and his entire family had put their trust in God; everyone in the house was in on the celebration.

READ

Read the passage aloud slowly, keeping in mind that just before this, Paul and Silas (after doing good) are stripped by a crowd, beaten black-and-blue by officials, and put in jail.

THINK

Read the passage again, noticing that this Bible version translates the word *saved* in these ways: "to really live" (verse 30) and "live as you were meant to live" (verse 31). The Greek word for "salvation" has to do with deliverance for the future but also living a new kind of life in the here and now.

1 Why do you think the jailer is so dramatically affected by Paul's and Silas's behavior?

2. Why would the jailer have an idea of what it meant to "put [his] entire trust in the Master Jesus"?

3. Picture these scenes:

   • the jailer making his prisoners feel at home with his family
   • the jailer dressing the wounds his coworkers had inflicted
   • Paul and Silas baptizing the family
   • the group eating a festive meal together, not knowing what would happen to Paul and Silas the next day

PRAY

Talk to God about what touches you most in this passage. What does that tell you about what you need from God? Ask God for that.

LIVE

Ponder the next twenty-four hours. In what area might you rejoice even though circumstances might not be happy? Who might you love who isn't expecting it? Watch for unexpected events and celebrate them.

NOT A GAME

ACTS 19:11-17

11-12   God did powerful things through Paul, things quite out of the ordinary. The word got around and people started taking pieces of clothing — handkerchiefs and scarves and the like — that had touched Paul's skin and then touching the sick with them. The touch did it — they were healed and whole.

13-16   Some itinerant Jewish exorcists who happened to be in town at the time tried their hand at what they assumed to be Paul's "game." They pronounced the name of the Master Jesus over victims of evil spirits, saying, "I command you by the Jesus preached by Paul!" The seven sons of a certain Sceva, a Jewish high priest, were trying to do this on a man when the evil spirit talked back: "I know Jesus and I've heard of Paul, but who are you?" Then the possessed man went berserk — jumped the exorcists, beat them up, and tore off their clothes. Naked and bloody, they got away as best they could.

17   It was soon news all over Ephesus among both Jews and Greeks. The realization spread that God was in and behind this. Curiosity about Paul developed into reverence for the Master Jesus.

READ
Read the passage.

THINK
Often God allows us to experience unpleasant consequences of choices we make, sometimes so we realize how our choices affect our relationship with him and other people. For example, he might allow ugly parts of our character to be exposed, with embarrassing and painful results. Why do you think God uses consequences to draw people's attention to the thorny parts of their hearts? What do you think God wanted the sons of Sceva to learn about themselves through this experience?

PRAY
Recall a difficult experience that helped you see more of your weaknesses or faults. Ponder the state of your relationship with God before the experience. How did it change? Think about your relationships with others, both before and after the experience. What changed? In other words, in what ways did your newfound awareness impact how you relate to others?

LIVE
Mull over these words, written by Teresa of Avila in her *Interior Castle*: "We are fonder of consolations than we are of the cross. Test us, Lord — for You know the truth — so that we may know ourselves."[4] Can you identify with her confession? Can you identify with her request to be more fully exposed to God and to see herself more clearly? Sit and talk with Jesus about your reaction to testing from God, contrasting it with your reaction to feel-good experiences.

FAITH JOURNEY

ACTS 22:1-10

1-2   "My dear brothers and fathers, listen carefully to what I have to say before you jump to conclusions about me." When they heard him speaking Hebrew, they grew even quieter. No one wanted to miss a word of this.

2-3   He continued, "I am a good Jew, born in Tarsus in the province of Cilicia, but educated here in Jerusalem under the exacting eye of Rabbi Gamaliel, thoroughly instructed in our religious traditions. And I've always been passionately on God's side, just as you are right now.

4-5   "I went after anyone connected with this 'Way,' went at them hammer and tongs, ready to kill for God. I rounded up men and women right and left and had them thrown in prison. You can ask the Chief Priest or anyone in the High Council to verify this; they all knew me well. Then I went off to our brothers in Damascus, armed with official documents authorizing me to hunt down the followers of Jesus there, arrest them, and bring them back to Jerusalem for sentencing.

6-7   "As I arrived on the outskirts of Damascus about noon, a blinding light blazed out of the skies and I fell to the ground, dazed. I heard a voice: 'Saul, Saul, why are you out to get me?'

8-9   "'Who are you, Master?' I asked.

"He said, 'I am Jesus the Nazarene, the One you're hunting down.' My companions saw the light, but they didn't hear the conversation.

10   "Then I said, 'What do I do now, Master?'

"He said, 'Get to your feet and enter Damascus. There you'll be told everything that's been set out for you to do.'"

READ

Read the passage from the perspective of Paul's mother. What might she be thinking as she hears these words?

THINK

Paul's faith began in an amazing way on the road to Damascus (see the beginning of Acts 9 for more details). He was bold to share his story and ultimately The Story, the one of God and man. This passage gives us a thorough yet succinct explanation of the person Paul was before he met Christ, how he met Christ, and the person he became after he met Christ.

Reflect on your story — how you came to faith and how your faith journey is continuing today. Who were you before Christ? What was meeting Christ like? In what ways is your life different now as a result of meeting him? Are other people different today because of your interaction with Jesus?

LIVE

Think about how you might describe your life-altering encounter with the Living God and your faith journey. Now write or type your story of faith in just two or three paragraphs. Finally, ask someone you know to help you hone it to include the most appropriate details.

PRAY

Pray that God will provide you an opportunity to present your story and The Story (of God and man) with another person in the next week. When you sense the open door plainly before you, take the risk and share the stories.

DAY 49

GOD ENCOUNTERS

On this seventh day, review and reflect on all you have read this week. Take the time to revel in the ways you've encountered God in the past six days.

WHY ARE YOU OUT TO GET ME?

ACTS 26:12-18

12-14 "One day on my way to Damascus, armed as always with papers from the high priests authorizing my action, right in the middle of the day a blaze of light, light outshining the sun, poured out of the sky on me and my companions. Oh, King, it was so bright! We fell flat on our faces. Then I heard a voice in Hebrew: 'Saul, Saul, why are you out to get me? Why do you insist on going against the grain?'

15-16 "I said, 'Who are you, Master?'

"The voice answered, 'I am Jesus, the One you're hunting down like an animal. But now, up on your feet—I have a job for you. I've handpicked you to be a servant and witness to what's happened today, and to what I am going to show you.

17-18 "'I'm sending you off to open the eyes of the outsiders so they can see the difference between dark and light, and choose light, see the difference between Satan and God, and choose God. I'm sending you off to present my offer of sins forgiven, and a place in the family, inviting them into the company of those who begin real living by believing in me.'"

READ

Read the passage aloud slowly. This is Paul speaking before King Agrippa, telling about his conversion.

THINK

Read the passage aloud again, this time noting all the personal pronouns in this very personal conversation: *I, me, you.*

Read it a third time, noting how the conversation focuses on the past and the future.

1. Why do you think Jesus doesn't just say, "I'm the Son of God. Your doctrine is wrong. Change it"?

2. How do you respond to Jesus' giving Saul a job to do even though he's been murdering Christians? What does this tell you about Jesus?

3. Consider what Paul might have prayed next; there he is, blind, with his underlings leading him to safety.

PRAY

Have a conversation with Jesus similar to Paul's.

First, Jesus asks you, "Why are you . . . ?" How do you respond?

Next, Jesus tells you exactly who he is — a glimpse of him you have missed: "I am Jesus the One you're . . ."

Finally, Jesus says, "Up on your feet — I have a job for you." What is the job? How do you respond?

Live today asking Jesus this question: *Is there anything about you I'm missing out on? That I don't understand or accept? Show me.*

PRIDE COMES BEFORE A FALL

ROMANS 2:17-24

17-24   If you're brought up Jewish, don't assume that you can lean back in the arms of your religion and take it easy, feeling smug because you're an insider to God's revelation, a connoisseur of the best things of God, informed on the latest doctrines! I have a special word of caution for you who are sure that you have it all together yourselves and, because you know God's revealed Word inside and out, feel qualified to guide others through their blind alleys and dark nights and confused emotions to God. While you are guiding others, who is going to guide you? I'm quite serious. While preaching "Don't steal!" are you going to rob people blind? Who would suspect you? The same with adultery. The same with idolatry. You can get by with almost anything if you front it with eloquent talk about God and his law. The line from Scripture, "It's because of you Jews that the outsiders are down on God," shows it's an old problem that isn't going to go away.

READ

Whisper to yourself the words of this passage.

THINK

Paul, writing mostly to Gentiles (non-Jews) in the church in Rome, finds himself addressing Jews in this passage, and warns those who have become arrogant because of their ancestral heritage. He warns that their arrogance, laziness, and apathy do not sit well with God. It leads to all sorts of thoughts and behaviors that dishonor God, including saying one thing and actually doing another.

You may or may not have Jewish roots, but this passage is relevant to all of us. What areas of your own heart might be arrogant or apathetic because of your upbringing, your heritage, or what you have done (and not done) in the past?

What might your friends who are far from God think or feel about this? What can be done about it?

When was the last time you said or taught one thing yet acted quite differently? What emotions might God feel when he sees us thinking or acting contrary to his character?

PRAY

Sit for a few minutes in silence, asking God to help you know the feeling of true humility. Then call on him to forgive you where your life has not lived up to what you claim to believe. (Be specific.)

LIVE

Courageously invite others around you to help you remain humble. Give them permission to do what it takes to help your life match your words.

TRUSTING WHEN IT'S HOPELESS

ROMANS 4:16-21

16   This is why the fulfillment of God's promise depends entirely on trusting God and his way, and then simply embracing him and what he does. God's promise arrives as pure gift. That's the only way everyone can be sure to get in on it, those who keep the religious traditions *and* those who have never heard of them. For Abraham is father of us all. He is not our racial father — that's reading the story backward. He is our *faith* father.

17-18   We call Abraham "father" not because he got God's attention by living like a saint, but because God made something out of Abraham when he was a nobody. Isn't that what we've always read in Scripture, God saying to Abraham, "I set you up as father of many peoples"? Abraham was first named "father" and then *became* a father because he dared to trust God to do what only God could do: raise the dead to life, with a word make something out of nothing. When everything was hopeless, Abraham believed anyway, deciding to live not on the basis of what he saw he *couldn't* do but on what God said he *would* do. And so he was made father of a multitude of peoples. God himself said to him, "You're going to have a big family, Abraham!"

19-21   Abraham didn't focus on his own impotence and say, "It's hopeless. This hundred-year-old body could never father a child." Nor did he survey Sarah's decades of infertility and give up. He didn't tiptoe around God's promise asking cautiously skeptical questions. He plunged into the promise and came up strong, ready for God, sure that God would make good on what he had said.

READ

Read the passage aloud slowly.

THINK

Read the passage again, but silently.

1. What did God do for Abraham?
2. If you were Abraham, which of the following efforts would be most difficult for you?

   ☐ daring to trust God to do what only God can do
   ☐ believing in spite of hopeless circumstances
   ☐ living on the basis of what God says he will do
   ☐ not focusing on hopeless circumstances
   ☐ not asking cautiously skeptical questions
   ☐ plunging into God's promise and coming up strong and ready for God
   ☐ remaining sure that God will make good on what he says
   ☐ other:

Read the passage again. What words or phrases stand out to you?

PRAY

Thank God for Abraham, "our *faith* father." Ask God to help you trust him and his way. Ask God to help you simply embrace him and what he does.

LIVE

Sit quietly before God. Get used to the idea that you really can embrace him and what he does. Imagine one way your life might be different if you do this.

SO-CALLED FREEDOM

ROMANS 6:15-21

15-18 So, since we're out from under the old tyranny, does that mean we can live any old way we want? Since we're free in the freedom of God, can we do anything that comes to mind? Hardly. You know well enough from your own experience that there are some acts of so-called freedom that destroy freedom. Offer yourselves to sin, for instance, and it's your last free act. But offer yourselves to the ways of God and the freedom never quits. All your lives you've let sin tell you what to do. But thank God you've started listening to a new master, one whose commands set you free to live openly in *his* freedom!

19 I'm using this freedom language because it's easy to picture. You can readily recall, can't you, how at one time the more you did just what you felt like doing — not caring about others, not caring about God — the worse your life became and the less freedom you had? And how much different is it now as you live in God's freedom, your lives healed and expansive in holiness?

20-21 As long as you did what you felt like doing, ignoring God, you didn't have to bother with right thinking or right living, or right *anything* for that matter. But do you call that a free life? What did you get out of it? Nothing you're proud of now. Where did it get you? A dead end.

THINK

Search yourself for an area where you don't walk in freedom but continue to struggle with sin. When do you easily give in to temptation? Why? Are there times when you don't feel the pull so strongly? Why? What comfort, relief, or pleasure does the sin give you (no matter how short-lived or shallow)? What pain or discomfort does it bring? What do you fear you would lose if you gave up the sin?

READ

Read the passage with your specific sin in mind. Sift these verses through your life experience. How do they hold up? Do you find Paul's description of living "any old way we want" to be accurate? What about his perspective on "offer[ing] yourselves to the ways of God"—living in obedience to his commands? Take time to identify what you do and don't agree with.

PRAY

Talk to God about the things you've uncovered. If you have unanswered questions or problems you can't reconcile, share them. If you're frustrated, express it to him. Maybe you will challenge him to show you freedom, as you agree to take on the challenge of giving his ways a shot.

LIVE

"Offer yourselves to the ways of God and the freedom never quits." Rest in this freedom today.

NOTHING BETWEEN US AND GOD'S LOVE

ROMANS 8:31-39

31-39   So, what do you think? With God on our side like this, how can we lose? If God didn't hesitate to put everything on the line for us, embracing our condition and exposing himself to the worst by sending his own Son, is there anything else he wouldn't gladly and freely do for us? And who would dare tangle with God by messing with one of God's chosen? Who would dare even to point a finger? The One who died for us — who was raised to life for us! — is in the presence of God at this very moment sticking up for us. Do you think anyone is going to be able to drive a wedge between us and Christ's love for us? There is no way! Not trouble, not hard times, not hatred, not hunger, not homelessness, not bullying threats, not backstabbing, not even the worst sins listed in Scripture:

> They kill us in cold blood because they hate you.
> We're sitting ducks; they pick us off one by one.

None of this fazes us because Jesus loves us. I'm absolutely convinced that nothing — nothing living or dead, angelic or demonic, today or tomorrow, high or low, thinkable or unthinkable — absolutely *nothing* can get between us and God's love because of the way that Jesus our Master has embraced us.

READ
Read the passage four times very slowly.

THINK
Logically understanding that God loves us is fairly easy. But grasping this truth to its fullest extent in our hearts and souls — in every corner of our everyday existence — requires more. We think we know God loves us, but we don't often ponder this profound truth, this important element of our identity as God's children.

Read the passage again. This time underline the phrases that speak directly to you and encourage your heart. With each underline, say aloud, "Thank you, God, for how much you love me."

"Do you think anyone is going to be able to drive a wedge between [you] and Christ's love for [you]? . . . No way!" When you read Paul's words, what flows through your mind and heart?

PRAY
Sit in silence with one thought in mind: *I am loved by God.* If your mind begins to wander, simply whisper, "Thank you for loving me, Jesus." Claim the promises of this passage as your own.

LIVE
Live confidently knowing that "absolutely *nothing* can get between [you] and God's love." He loves you that much!

EMBRACE GOD, HEART AND SOUL

ROMANS 10:8-13

8-10   So what exactly was Moses saying?

> The word that saves is right here,
>   as near as the tongue in your mouth,
>   as close as the heart in your chest.

It's the word of faith that welcomes God to go to work and set things right for us. This is the core of our preaching. Say the welcoming word to God — "Jesus is my Master" — embracing, body and soul, God's work of doing in us what he did in raising Jesus from the dead. That's it. You're not "doing" anything; you're simply calling out to God, trusting him to do it for you. That's salvation. With your whole being you embrace God setting things right, and then you say it, right out loud: "God has set everything right between him and me!"

11-13   Scripture reassures us, "No one who trusts God like this — heart and soul — will ever regret it." It's exactly the same no matter what a person's religious background may be: the same God for all of us, acting the same incredibly generous way to everyone who calls out for help. "Everyone who calls, 'Help, God!' gets help."

READ

Read the passage aloud slowly.

THINK

Read the passage again silently.

1. Look at the rich phrases and see which one speaks to you most:

   ☐ "the word . . . as near as the tongue . . . as close as the heart"
   ☐ "the word of faith that welcomes God to go to work"
   ☐ "embracing, body and soul, God's work of doing in us what he did in raising Jesus"
   ☐ "calling out to God"
   ☐ "God has set everything right between him and me!"
   ☐ "No one who trusts God like this — heart and soul — will ever regret it."
   ☐ "Everyone who calls, 'Help, God!' gets help."

2. Why does this phrase touch you?
3. In what way would you like this phrase to become a stronger reality in your life?

PRAY

Thank God for his nearness, his willingness to be embraced, his willingness to hear us and set things right. Talk to God about your next step in trusting him heart and soul.

LIVE

Sit quietly before God, imagining what it feels like to live trusting him and embracing him — a life without regret.

DAY 56

GOD ENCOUNTERS

On this seventh day, review and reflect on all you have read this week. Take the time to revel in the ways you've encountered God in the past six days.

AN OFFERING

ROMANS 12:1-3

1-2 So here's what I want you to do, God helping you: Take your everyday, ordinary life — your sleeping, eating, going-to-work, and walking-around life — and place it before God as an offering. Embracing what God does for you is the best thing you can do for him. Don't become so well-adjusted to your culture that you fit into it without even thinking. Instead, fix your attention on God. You'll be changed from the inside out. Readily recognize what he wants from you, and quickly respond to it. Unlike the culture around you, always dragging you down to its level of immaturity, God brings the best out of you, develops well-formed maturity in you.

3 I'm speaking to you out of deep gratitude for all that God has given me, and especially as I have responsibilities in relation to you. Living then, as every one of you does, in pure grace, it's important that you not misinterpret yourselves as people who are bringing this goodness to God. No, God brings it all to you. The only accurate way to understand ourselves is by what God is and by what he does for us, not by what we are and what we do for him.

READ
Read the passage twice, aloud.

THINK
Choose a theme that speaks to you — perhaps the idea that God is the real source of goodness in your life or perhaps the contrast Paul makes between what your culture draws out in you and what God draws out in you. What does this passage say about that issue?

PRAY
Pick one phrase from the passage that pinpoints the theme that impacts you. Repeat that phrase to yourself slowly several times. Each time you say it, notice your internal response. What thoughts, memories, or feelings does it stir up?

Now bring these thoughts back to the passage, line by line, in a conversation with God: He speaks to you through the words in the passage, then you respond to what he said. (For example, if you feel the power of your culture is "dragging you down," you bring that feeling to each line of the passage and see how God replies.) When you're finished, repeat the phrase to yourself one last time, checking your heart's reaction. Is it different? Don't worry if this process leaves unanswered questions. Just be open to what God is showing you through your meditation.

LIVE
Consider one of the four "everyday, ordinary" parts of your life suggested in the passage: sleeping, eating, going to work, walking around. What would placing this activity before God as an offering look like? How would you think about this activity differently? Would the frequency, method, or other details of your activity change? Try it today.

GOVERNMENT AND GOD

ROMANS 13:1-7

1-3 Be a good citizen. All governments are under God. Insofar as there is peace and order, it's God's order. So live responsibly as a citizen. If you're irresponsible to the state, then you're irresponsible with God, and God will hold you responsible. Duly constituted authorities are only a threat if you're trying to get by with something. Decent citizens should have nothing to fear.

3-5 Do you want to be on good terms with the government? Be a responsible citizen and you'll get on just fine, the government working to your advantage. But if you're breaking the rules right and left, watch out. The police aren't there just to be admired in their uniforms. God also has an interest in keeping order, and he uses them to do it. That's why you must live responsibly — not just to avoid punishment but also because it's the right way to live.

6-7 That's also why you pay taxes — so that an orderly way of life can be maintained. Fulfill your obligations as a citizen. Pay your taxes, pay your bills, respect your leaders.

THINK

There are all sorts of opinions out there regarding how our government should be run. And people have a hard time talking about church and government in the same paragraphs. *Separation of church and state,* we think.

But when was the last time you thanked God for people in office or prayed for their leadership? Have you ever thought about the truth that God is powerful and in control of the world in such a way that he is not surprised by who is in office, regardless of that person's political views?

In this passage, Paul commands, "Fulfill your obligations as a citizen. Pay your taxes, pay your bills, respect your leaders." What is your obligation as a citizen to this country and to the kingdom of God? In what specific ways can you respect your leaders?

READ

Read the passage.

PRAY

Find a list of names of your local officials (mayor, city council members, county officials), as well as your state and federal officials (governor, congressmen and women, senators, Supreme Court justices, vice president, and president). Pray for each one of them by name. Pray that God would use them to lead wisely and justly.

LIVE

Consider writing a short note or letter of encouragement to one or two of the government officials you prayed for, telling them you are thankful for what they do.

DEBATABLE MATTERS

ROMANS 14:6-10,13

6-9 What's important in all this is that if you keep a holy day, keep it for *God's* sake; if you eat meat, eat it to the glory of God and thank God for prime rib; if you're a vegetarian, eat vegetables to the glory of God and thank God for broccoli. None of us are permitted to insist on our own way in these matters. It's *God* we are answerable to — all the way from life to death and everything in between — not each other. That's why Jesus lived and died and then lived again: so that he could be our Master across the entire range of life and death, and free us from the petty tyrannies of each other.

10 So where does that leave you when you criticize a brother? And where does that leave you when you condescend to a sister? I'd say it leaves you looking pretty silly — or worse. Eventually, we're all going to end up kneeling side by side in the place of judgment, facing God. Your critical and condescending ways aren't going to improve your position there one bit. . . .

13 Forget about deciding what's right for each other. Here's what you need to be concerned about: that you don't get in the way of someone else, making life more difficult than it already is.

READ

Read the passage aloud slowly, keeping in mind that Paul has been addressing a controversy about what foods are right to eat.

THINK

Read the passage aloud again, imagining that Paul, your brother in Christ, is sitting next to you in a window seat, saying these things to you.

1. Why do people insist on their own way about debatable matters?
2. When you're critical, what words and tone do you usually use? When you're being condescending, what facial expression and arm gestures do you use?
3. What does this passage say about why moral superiority is so silly?

Read the passage aloud again. Which phrase speaks most deeply to you?

PRAY

Take the phrase that spoke to you and talk to God about it. Ask him to let that truth sink into your deepest self. Ask him to guide you in that truth.

LIVE

When Mother Teresa was asked how someone might pray for her, she asked that person to pray that she would not get in the way of what God wanted to do. Move through life with that consciousness, acting with God's love but not getting in the way of what God wants to do.

STRENGTH IS FOR SERVICE

ROMANS 15:1-6

1-2 Those of us who are strong and able in the faith need to step in and lend a hand to those who falter, and not just do what is most convenient for us. Strength is for service, not status. Each one of us needs to look after the good of the people around us, asking ourselves, "How can I help?"

3-6 That's exactly what Jesus did. He didn't make it easy for himself by avoiding people's troubles, but waded right in and helped out. "I took on the troubles of the troubled," is the way Scripture puts it. Even if it was written in Scripture long ago, you can be sure it's written for *us*. God wants the combination of his steady, constant calling and warm, personal counsel in Scripture to come to characterize *us*, keeping us alert for whatever he will do next. May our dependably steady and warmly personal God develop maturity in you so that you get along with each other as well as Jesus gets along with us all. Then we'll be a choir — not our voices only, but our very lives singing in harmony in a stunning anthem to the God and Father of our Master Jesus!

THINK

Paul specifies that we are to help others in areas where we are "strong and able in the faith." What are some areas in which you have received training, direction, or guidance? What are some of your natural gifts and strengths?

READ

Read the passage with a heart of gratitude for those who, past and present, "step in and lend a hand" to you, even if you don't remember specific details.

PRAY

Ponder what this passage says about Jesus and how he dealt with people's troubles. Now think about his call to follow him (see Matthew 16:24). When you think about being like Jesus in this way, what questions, thoughts, and feelings come up? Share these with him.

LIVE

Contemplate the role that service to others plays in your daily life. There are a variety of forms this might take, for example, lending a listening ear or emotional support, doing manual labor or other chores for someone, or giving money, food, shelter, or clothing to a person in need. Has your service to others become another form of overwork? Or is it truly integrated into your life in a comfortable and valuable way? Have you been selfish in the use of your time? Should you be giving more of yourself to others than you currently do?[5]

CALLED INTO THIS LIFE

1 CORINTHIANS 1:26-31

26-31 Take a good look, friends, at who you were when you got called into this life. I don't see many of "the brightest and the best" among you, not many influential, not many from high-society families. Isn't it obvious that God deliberately chose men and women that the culture overlooks and exploits and abuses, chose these "nobodies" to expose the hollow pretensions of the "somebodies"? That makes it quite clear that none of you can get by with blowing your own horn before God. Everything that we have — right thinking and right living, a clean slate and a fresh start — comes from God by way of Jesus Christ. That's why we have the saying, "If you're going to blow a horn, blow a trumpet for God."

READ

Ruminate over these verses. Take your time and read them slowly.

THINK

What sticks out to you in this passage concerning God and your relationship with him?

When have you tried to "get by with blowing your own horn before God," either overtly or subtly?

Consider the entire story of Scripture, starting with Genesis. Think about the types of people God fights for and the types he uses to impact human history: Abraham, Moses, Gideon, Saul (later Paul), Peter, and so on. Many of them started out inadequate or less-than-qualified for the job. How does this make you feel about God's desire to use you in his grand plan for the world?

PRAY

Write down your thoughts and prayers in these two areas:

1. "Take a good look, friends, at who you were when you got called into this life." Think about what your life was like — specifically and generally — before meeting Christ. (If you don't remember because you let Christ in when you were really young, think about the person you were even five years ago.)
2. Reflect on the person you are today — the ways you are different due to God's involvement in your life.

Thank God for what he's done.

LIVE

Live confidently today, knowing that God wants to use you — yes, even you — for his ultimate purpose and plan. Live openly before him, realizing that you are an instrument in a world desperately in need of hope.

YOU ARE A TEMPLE

1 CORINTHIANS 3:11-17

11-15   Remember, there is only one foundation, the one already laid: Jesus Christ. Take particular care in picking out your building materials. Eventually there is going to be an inspection. If you use cheap or inferior materials, you'll be found out. The inspection will be thorough and rigorous. You won't get by with a thing. If your work passes inspection, fine; if it doesn't, your part of the building will be torn out and started over. But *you* won't be torn out; you'll survive — but just barely.

16-17   You realize, don't you, that you are the temple of God, and God himself is present in you? No one will get by with vandalizing God's temple, you can be sure of that. God's temple is sacred — and you, remember, *are* the temple.

READ

Read the passage aloud slowly.

THINK

Read it aloud again, imagining Paul speaking to you as a good father would speak to you (see 1 Corinthians 4:14-17).

In the metaphor where each of us is a building, Jesus is the foundation. What "cheap or inferior materials" might someone use for their foundation? (In general, this would be anything other than Jesus, but be specific for yourself and others like you.)

The sort of building that you are is a temple. A temple is where people go to pray. Not only is God himself present in the temple (you), but both the Holy Spirit and Jesus also live inside you and intercede for you (see Romans 8:26-27,34). What might you do to keep your temple a sacred space?

Read the passage again silently. What does it make you want to be or do or entrust to God?

PRAY

Talk to God about your being a temple for him — even celebrate it! Then ask what you need to know and do to make the Trinity feel at home inside you.

LIVE

Move through life today, musing to yourself about truly being a temple in which the Trinity dwells. Do something to celebrate that.

DAY 63

GOD ENCOUNTERS

On this seventh day, review and reflect on all you have read this week. Take the time to revel in the ways you've encountered God in the past six days.

NO SMALL THING

1 CORINTHIANS 5:1-6

1-2   I also received a report of scandalous sex within your church family, a kind that wouldn't be tolerated even outside the church: One of your men is sleeping with his stepmother. And you're so above it all that it doesn't even faze you! Shouldn't this break your hearts? Shouldn't it bring you to your knees in tears? Shouldn't this person and his conduct be confronted and dealt with?

3-5   I'll tell you what I would do. Even though I'm not there in person, consider me right there with you, because I can fully see what's going on. I'm telling you that this is wrong. You must not simply look the other way and hope it goes away on its own. Bring it out in the open and deal with it in the authority of Jesus our Master. Assemble the community — I'll be present in spirit with you and our Master Jesus will be present in power. Hold this man's conduct up to public scrutiny. Let him defend it if he can! But if he can't, then out with him! It will be totally devastating to him, of course, and embarrassing to you. But better devastation and embarrassment than damnation. You want him on his feet and forgiven before the Master on the Day of Judgment.

6   Your flip and callous arrogance in these things bothers me. You pass it off as a small thing, but it's anything but that. Yeast, too, is a "small thing," but it works its way through a whole batch of bread dough pretty fast.

READ

Read the passage.

THINK

Have you ever observed the process of baking bread? By the work of a pinch of yeast, a small ball of dough doubles in size. Consider how this process is similar to what happens with sin and tolerance among Christians. In what way does "flip and callous arrogance" make the problem worse?

PRAY

Think of a particular experience you've had with sin lately — either your own or that of someone you're close to. How did you respond? Did the sin break your heart? Did you confront it? Did you avoid or ignore it?

Picture Jesus sitting with you. Talk to him about what happened. Explore your heart with him and ask him to uncover why you responded the way you did.

LIVE

Consider this statement by Julian of Norwich: "[God] comes down to the lowest part of our need. For he never despises that which he himself has made."[6] Do you believe it's true about you? About others you know? Write down what this touches in you and anything you sense God is inviting you to do in response.

RISKING SOMEONE'S ETERNAL RUIN

1 CORINTHIANS 8:7-9

7   In strict logic, then, nothing happened to the meat when it was offered up to an idol. It's just like any other meat. I know that, and you know that. But knowing isn't everything. If it becomes everything, some people end up as know-it-alls who treat others as know-nothings. Real knowledge isn't that insensitive.

  We need to be sensitive to the fact that we're not all at the same level of understanding in this. Some of you have spent your entire lives eating "idol meat," and are sure that there's something bad in the meat that then becomes something bad inside of you. An imagination and conscience shaped under those conditions isn't going to change overnight.

8-9   But fortunately God doesn't grade us on our diet. We're neither commended when we clean our plate nor reprimanded when we just can't stomach it. But God *does* care when you use your freedom carelessly in a way that leads a fellow believer still vulnerable to those old associations to be thrown off track.

READ

This passage was part of an actual letter. Pretend you have just pulled this letter from your mailbox. Read the words as though they are handwritten by a friend.

THINK

Paul gives instruction here to the church in Corinth regarding meat sacrificed to idols. Translated to our current culture, this instruction would be similar to Christians who believe that people should never drink alcohol versus Christians who believe that people have the freedom to drink alcohol, depending on their maturity in their Christian walk. Paul says, "We need to be sensitive to the fact that we're not all at the same level of understanding in this."

Think of a situation when you could have been more sensitive to other believers who may have a different understanding than you. How can you grow to be more sensitive to others without becoming soft on the truth? What sacrifices in your own life need to be made to ensure you aren't tripping up other believers?

Where is the limit on our freedom in Christ?

PRAY

Ask God to search your heart in the area of sensitive interaction with other believers. Consider not only *what* you say or do but also *how* you say or do it. Ask the Holy Spirit to give you wisdom and compassion for healthy, God-honoring relationships with other believers.

Finally, ask God to show you if there is anyone you need to request forgiveness from due to an interaction that involved differing views on these types of issues.

LIVE

If applicable, boldly but humbly seek out those individuals and their forgiveness for your lack of sensitivity. Consider also talking with friends or family members in the near future about what freedom in Christ expressed appropriately might look like.

EXPERIENCING GOD'S WONDER AND GRACE

1 CORINTHIANS 10:1-10

1-5 Remember our history, friends, and be warned. All our ancestors were led by the providential Cloud and taken miraculously through the Sea. They went through the waters, in a baptism like ours, as Moses led them from enslaving death to salvation life. They all ate and drank identical food and drink, meals provided daily by God. They drank from the Rock, God's fountain for them that stayed with them wherever they were. And the Rock was Christ. But just experiencing God's wonder and grace didn't seem to mean much — most of them were defeated by temptation during the hard times in the desert, and God was not pleased.

6-10 The same thing could happen to us. We must be on guard so that we never get caught up in wanting our own way as they did. And we must not turn our religion into a circus as they did — "First the people partied, then they threw a dance." We must not be sexually promiscuous — they paid for that, remember, with 23,000 deaths in one day! We must never try to get Christ to serve us instead of us serving him; they tried it, and God launched an epidemic of poisonous snakes. We must be careful not to stir up discontent; discontent destroyed them.

READ

Read the passage aloud slowly, realizing that Paul is referring to how the Israelites exited Egypt, crossed the Red Sea, and journeyed to the Promised Land.

THINK

Read the passage again.

1. What miracles did the Israelites experience? (Note: Some people read verse 4 to mean that the same rock followed them or appeared at each of their resting places — and "the Rock was Christ." So Christ journeyed with them.)
2. "Just experiencing God's wonder and grace didn't seem to mean much" to the Israelites. Try to understand and explain how they could have developed this attitude.
3. Which of these ways that the Israelites wanted their own way captivates you most?

   ☐ turning religion into a circus — partying and dancing
   ☐ being sexually promiscuous
   ☐ trying to get Christ to serve us instead of serving him
   ☐ stirring up discontent (or maybe just not dealing with it)

PRAY

Read the passage one more time. Thank God that he draws you to experience his wonder and grace every day. Ask him to keep you away from temptation and to teach you how to deal with it.

LIVE

Be alert and expectant today, noticing God's wonder and grace, and thanking him for it. See yourself as learning from the Israelites' mistakes.

MY BODY, BROKEN FOR YOU

1 CORINTHIANS 11:23-29

23-26   Let me go over with you again exactly what goes on in the Lord's Supper and why it is so centrally important. I received my instructions from the Master himself and passed them on to you. The Master, Jesus, on the night of his betrayal, took bread. Having given thanks, he broke it and said,

> This is my body, broken for you.
> Do this to remember me.

After supper, he did the same thing with the cup:
> This cup is my blood, my new covenant with you.
> Each time you drink this cup, remember me.

What you must solemnly realize is that every time you eat this bread and every time you drink this cup, you reenact in your words and actions the death of the Master. You will be drawn back to this meal again and again until the Master returns. You must never let familiarity breed contempt.

27-28   Anyone who eats the bread or drinks the cup of the Master irreverently is like part of the crowd that jeered and spit on him at his death. Is that the kind of "remembrance" you want to be part of? Examine your motives, test your heart, come to this meal in holy awe.

29   If you give no thought (or worse, don't care) about the broken body of the Master when you eat and drink, you're running the risk of serious consequences.

THINK

Briefly think back on the last time you took Communion. What was it like for you? Did it feel routine or special? In what ways? Who was there with you? Did the presence of that person(s) change the experience for you in any way? How did you prepare yourself?

READ

Read the passage, being especially aware of how you usually approach Communion.

PRAY

Be aware of the Holy Spirit's presence with you now. Meditate on what stands out to you in Paul's description of the communion experience. What is your reaction to his words? Do you resonate with his serious tone? Do you feel challenged by anything in particular? Invite the Holy Spirit to examine your heart and to filter out any junk he finds there — and make you clean.

LIVE

Take time to examine your heart now, as at Communion. What do you need to clear up with God? With another person? Meditate on this Anglican prayer from the *Book of Common Prayer* (1979): "We do not presume to come to this thy Table, O merciful Lord, trusting in our own righteousness, but in thy manifold and great mercies. We are not worthy so much as to gather up the crumbs under thy Table. But thou art the same Lord whose property is always to have mercy. Grant us therefore, gracious Lord, so to eat the flesh of thy dear Son Jesus Christ, and to drink his blood, that we may evermore dwell in him, and he in us. *Amen*."[7]

Find out the next time your church plans to offer Communion, and set aside time on your calendar to revisit this prayer of examination before you participate.

BANKRUPT WITHOUT LOVE

1 CORINTHIANS 13:3-7

3-7   If I give everything I own to the poor and even go to the stake to be burned as a martyr, but I don't love, I've gotten nowhere. So, no matter what I say, what I believe, and what I do, I'm bankrupt without love.

> Love never gives up.
> Love cares more for others than for self.
> Love doesn't want what it doesn't have.
> Love doesn't strut,
> Doesn't have a swelled head,
> Doesn't force itself on others,
> Isn't always "me first,"
> Doesn't fly off the handle,
> Doesn't keep score of the sins of others,
> Doesn't revel when others grovel,
> Takes pleasure in the flowering of truth,
> Puts up with anything,
> Trusts God always,
> Always looks for the best,
> Never looks back,
> But keeps going to the end.

READ

Ask God to give you fresh insight into these familiar words, allowing you to learn things that you haven't before. Now read the passage.

THINK

Whether we know Scripture well or not, most of us have heard this passage read during a wedding ceremony. Its words are encouraging and uplifting, and we might hope the couple won't forget them (and us either). But as you know, reading the words is much easier than living by them.

Ponder this sentence: "So, no matter what I say, what I believe, and what I do, I'm bankrupt without love." What specifically does this mean in your own life?

Consider the list that defines love. Read line by line, asking yourself these two questions: In what ways am I living this out well? In what ways do I need to improve?

PRAY

Pick the one that needs more improvement, and communicate it to God. Ask him to remodel your life in such a way that you quickly see changes in this area. Ask for the ability to recognize when you're not exemplifying the godly love described in this passage.

LIVE

Someplace where you will see it often today — in your PDA, on your hand, or at the top of a notebook — write the one way you want to improve. When you see it, ask yourself how you might express that attribute to those around you.

DON'T HOLD BACK

1 CORINTHIANS 15:51-58

51-57 But let me tell you something wonderful, a mystery I'll probably never fully understand. We're not all going to die — *but* we are all going to be changed. You hear a blast to end all blasts from a trumpet, and in the time that you look up and blink your eyes — it's over. On signal from that trumpet from heaven, the dead will be up and out of their graves, beyond the reach of death, never to die again. At the same moment and in the same way, we'll all be changed. In the resurrection scheme of things, this has to happen: everything perishable taken off the shelves and replaced by the imperishable, this mortal replaced by the immortal. Then the saying will come true:

> Death swallowed by triumphant Life!
> Who got the last word, oh, Death?
> Oh, Death, who's afraid of you now?

It was sin that made death so frightening and law-code guilt that gave sin its leverage, its destructive power. But now in a single victorious stroke of Life, all three — sin, guilt, death — are gone, the gift of our Master, Jesus Christ. Thank God!

58 With all this going for us, my dear, dear friends, stand your ground. And don't hold back. Throw yourselves into the work of the Master, confident that nothing you do for him is a waste of time or effort.

READ

Read this passage a few times, slowly and meditatively.

THINK

What phrase or idea in this passage stands out to you? Perhaps you are drawn toward the "blast to end all blasts" or being free from the fear of death, or maybe you are more drawn to the concept of not holding back in your work. Allow this idea to unfold in your mind. What does it mean for your life today?

PRAY

Talk to the Master about how this makes you feel. If you have questions for him, don't hold on to them: Let Jesus hear them and then let them go. Trust that your questions will be answered at the right time.

Once you have shared your concerns with Jesus, sit with him in silence, being open to whatever he might say in response.

LIVE

Consider Paul's instruction to the Christians in Corinth to "throw [them]-selves into the work of the Master." Ponder: What is the "work" you have been made for? Consider your interests, abilities, skills, passions. When do you feel most alive? (The work you've been made for may or may not correspond to your current vocation.)

What holds you back from pursuing this work with your whole heart — however that might look at this stage in your life? Consider the legitimate reasons, as well as the reasons that might be illegitimate but are still preventing you from moving ahead. Talk to God about this. Ask him to show you what he would have you do, even if that's the simple step of waiting on him to slowly reveal your work over time.

DAY 70

GOD ENCOUNTERS

On this seventh day, review and reflect on all you have read this week. Take the time to revel in the ways you've encountered God in the past six days.

DAY 71
EXPANDED PASSAGE: 2 CORINTHIANS 1–2

YES!

2 CORINTHIANS 1:17-22

17-19   Are you now going to accuse me of being flip with my promises because it didn't work out? Do you think I talk out of both sides of my mouth — a glib *yes* one moment, a glib *no* the next? Well, you're wrong. I try to be as true to my word as God is to his. Our word to you wasn't a careless yes canceled by an indifferent no. How could it be? When Silas and Timothy and I proclaimed the Son of God among you, did you pick up on any yes-and-no, on-again, off-again waffling? Wasn't it a clean, strong Yes?

20-22   Whatever God has promised gets stamped with the Yes of Jesus. In him, this is what we preach and pray, the great Amen, God's Yes and our Yes together, gloriously evident. God affirms us, making us a sure thing in Christ, putting his Yes within us. By his Spirit he has stamped us with his eternal pledge — a sure beginning of what he is destined to complete.

READ

Read the passage slowly, at least three times.

THINK

In these verses, Paul writes to the church in the city of Corinth about the promises of God through the fulfillment of Jesus. Read the passage again and circle the word *yes* each time it appears in the text.

So often we hear the word *no,* but this passage says, "God affirms us, making us a sure thing in Christ, putting his Yes with us." What does it mean to hear *yes* from God?

What would your life look like (specifically) if you allowed "God's Yes and [y]our Yes together, gloriously evident"?

PRAY

Allow God to affirm you as you simply sit with him.

Invite him to bring his promises of "yes" to your mind and heart. What specific promises has he given to you? Embrace those promises and ask him to place these stamps of "yes" on your heart so you can carry them with you.

LIVE

Write down one or two specific "yeses" God has given you. Carry that note around with you. Consider sharing these promises with a friend, roommate, family member, classmate, or coworker today.

LIFTING THE VEIL

2 CORINTHIANS 3:12-18

12-15 With that kind of hope to excite us, nothing holds us back. Unlike Moses, we have nothing to hide. Everything is out in the open with us. He wore a veil so the children of Israel wouldn't notice that the glory was fading away — and they *didn't* notice. They didn't notice it then and they don't notice it now, don't notice that there's nothing left behind that veil. Even today when the proclamations of that old, bankrupt government are read out, they can't see through it. Only Christ can get rid of the veil so they can see for themselves that there's nothing there.

16-18 Whenever, though, they turn to face God as Moses did, God removes the veil and there they are — face-to-face! They suddenly recognize that God is a living, personal presence, not a piece of chiseled stone. And when God is personally present, a living Spirit, that old, constricting legislation is recognized as obsolete. We're free of it! All of us! Nothing between us and God, our faces shining with the brightness of his face. And so we are transfigured much like the Messiah, our lives gradually becoming brighter and more beautiful as God enters our lives and we become like him.

READ

Read the passage aloud slowly.

THINK

Again, slowly read verses 12-15 with a mood of despair. Then read verses 16-18 with a mood of joy, mystery, and surprise.

1. What words or phrases stand out to you? Why?
2. If you didn't choose words or phrases from verses 16-18, do that now. Read them again and note the frequency of these words: *face, personal, personally, bright, brighter, brightness.*

PRAY

Paraphrase verses 16-18 back to God, something like: Whenever I turn my face to you, O God, you remove the veil and there we are — face-to-face! I will suddenly recognize you as a living, personal presence, not [fill in, perhaps: a remote, unknown figure]. And when you are personally present, a living Spirit, that old, constricting legalism is recognized as obsolete. I'm free of it! All of us are! Nothing between me and you, my face shining with the brightness of your face. And so I am transfigured much like the Messiah. My life gradually becomes brighter and more beautiful as you enter my life and I become like you.

LIVE

Sit quietly before God, basking in one of these phrases:

- you are "a living, personal presence"
- nothing between you and me
- as you enter my life, it gradually becomes brighter and more beautiful

OUR ORDINARY LIVES

2 CORINTHIANS 4:5-13

5-6 Remember, our Message is not about ourselves; we're proclaiming Jesus Christ, the Master. All we are is messengers, errand runners from Jesus for you. It started when God said, "Light up the darkness!" and our lives filled up with light as we saw and understood God in the face of Christ, all bright and beautiful.

7-12 If you only look at *us*, you might well miss the brightness. We carry this precious Message around in the unadorned clay pots of our ordinary lives. That's to prevent anyone from confusing God's incomparable power with us. As it is, there's not much chance of that. You know for yourselves that we're not much to look at. We've been surrounded and battered by troubles, but we're not demoralized; we're not sure what to do, but we know that God knows what to do; we've been spiritually terrorized, but God hasn't left our side; we've been thrown down, but we haven't broken. What they did to Jesus, they do to us — trial and torture, mockery and murder; what Jesus did among them, he does in us — he lives! Our lives are at constant risk for Jesus' sake, which makes Jesus' life all the more evident in us. While we're going through the worst, you're getting in on the best!

13 We're not keeping this quiet, not on your life. Just like the psalmist who wrote, "I believed it, so I said it," we say what we believe.

READ

Read the passage aloud once. Read it a second time, and if a word catches your attention, stop and toss it around in your mind. Listen briefly for what your heart is saying in reply. Then keep reading.

THINK

In the silence that follows your reading, meditate on what you heard. How do you relate to the troubled, terrorized, and battered lifestyle Paul and other Christians in the first century led? If you can't relate, what other people around you might be run-down and struggling?

PRAY

Tell God what you've been thinking about. What is your response to the trouble and pain in or around you? If it's your own pain, share with God what you wish you could do in response. If it's the pain of another, notice your impulse to help, fix, or ignore. Be open to God's response to you. Let your sharing lead you into a silent prayer of thankfulness, humility, or request.

LIVE

In her book *Going on Retreat,* Margaret Silf describes what she calls a "retreat on the streets": Small groups of people meet to pray, then they go off into the city with only a few dollars to spend on food that day, taking opportunities to talk with the homeless, unemployed, disturbed, or addicted. At the end of the day, the group gathers to share thoughts and feelings, and to pray.[8]

While this kind of retreat may not be appropriate for you at this time, think about how you could intentionally seek to engage with the needs and feelings of disadvantaged people around you. What would your "ordinary life" look like if you let the light within you shine amid the darkness?

A FRESH START

2 CORINTHIANS 5:14-21

14-15   Our firm decision is to work from this focused center: One man died for everyone. That puts everyone in the same boat. He included everyone in his death so that everyone could also be included in his life, a resurrection life, a far better life than people ever lived on their own.

16-20   Because of this decision we don't evaluate people by what they have or how they look. We looked at the Messiah that way once and got it all wrong, as you know. We certainly don't look at him that way anymore. Now we look inside, and what we see is that anyone united with the Messiah gets a fresh start, is created new. The old life is gone; a new life burgeons! Look at it! All this comes from the God who settled the relationship between us and him, and then called us to settle our relationships with each other. God put the world square with himself through the Messiah, giving the world a fresh start by offering forgiveness of sins. God has given us the task of telling everyone what he is doing. We're Christ's representatives. God uses us to persuade men and women to drop their differences and enter into God's work of making things right between them. We're speaking for Christ himself now: Become friends with God; he's already a friend with you.

21   How? you ask. In Christ. God put the wrong on him who never did anything wrong, so we could be put right with God.

READ

Read the passage.

THINK

What implications does this passage have for your life right now?

Meditate on these words: "Now we look inside, and what we see is that anyone united with the Messiah gets a fresh start, is created new. The old life is gone; a new life burgeons!" (You might consider their radical inclusiveness.)

"Become friends with God; he's already a friend with you." How can you become a better friend to God? What would that entail? How does it feel to know that God is already a friend to you? Do you feel deserving of his friendship? Why or why not?

PRAY

Thank God that he gives you a fresh start with your life and a fresh start every single morning. Let your thankfulness spill over; tell God that you are grateful to have new life in him.

Ask God to help you become a better friend to him and to help you understand what a friend he is to you!

LIVE

"God has given us the task of telling everyone what he is doing. We're Christ's representatives." Who can you tell today about what God is doing in the world?

A WIDE-OPEN, SPACIOUS LIFE

2 CORINTHIANS 6:1-13

1-10 Companions as we are in this work with you, we beg you, please don't squander one bit of this marvelous life God has given us. God reminds us,

> I heard your call in the nick of time;
> The day you needed me, I was there to help.

Well, now is the right time to listen, the day to be helped. Don't put it off; don't frustrate God's work by showing up late, throwing a question mark over everything we're doing. Our work as God's servants gets validated — or not — in the details. People are watching us as we stay at our post, alertly, unswervingly . . . in hard times, tough times, bad times; when we're beaten up, jailed, and mobbed; working hard, working late, working without eating; with pure heart, clear head, steady hand; in gentleness, holiness, and honest love; when we're telling the truth, and when God's showing his power; when we're doing our best setting things right; when we're praised, and when we're blamed; slandered, and honored; true to our word, though distrusted; ignored by the world, but recognized by God; terrifically alive, though rumored to be dead; beaten within an inch of our lives, but refusing to die; immersed in tears, yet always filled with deep joy; living on handouts, yet enriching many; having nothing, having it all.

11-13 Dear, dear Corinthians, I can't tell you how much I long for you to enter this wide-open, spacious life. We didn't fence you in. The smallness you feel comes from within you. Your lives aren't small, but you're living them in a small way. I'm speaking as plainly as I can and with great affection. Open up your lives. Live openly and expansively!

READ

Read the passage aloud slowly.

THINK

Read the passage again, noting these words (and their various forms): *work, working; life, living, lives, alive.*

1. What does this passage have to say to someone who thinks life is boring?
2. What does it say to someone who thinks living for God is boring?
3. With what sort of heart did Paul and his friends do their work for God?

Read the passage one more time — very slowly.

4. What words or phrases are most meaningful to you?
5. How do they connect with your life right now?

PRAY

Talk to God about the opportunity to live a "wide-open, spacious life." Ask him to show you how to work hard with a heart of "gentleness, holiness, and honest love," and with a life of power and joy.

LIVE

Sit in the word *live*. Picture yourself fully alive, partnering with God in what he is doing (or wants to do) in you, and in the people and circumstances around you.

DISTRESS THAT DRIVES US TO GOD

2 CORINTHIANS 7:8-13

8-9 I know I distressed you greatly with my letter. Although I felt awful at the time, I don't feel at all bad now that I see how it turned out. The letter upset you, but only for a while. Now I'm glad — not that you were upset, but that you were jarred into turning things around. You let the distress bring you to God, not drive you from him. The result was all gain, no loss.

10 Distress that drives us to God does that. It turns us around. It gets us back in the way of salvation. We never regret that kind of pain. But those who let distress drive them away from God are full of regrets, end up on a deathbed of regrets.

11-13 And now, isn't it wonderful all the ways in which this distress has goaded you closer to God? You're more alive, more concerned, more sensitive, more reverent, more human, more passionate, more responsible. Looked at from any angle, you've come out of this with purity of heart. And that is what I was hoping for in the first place when I wrote the letter. My primary concern was not for the one who did the wrong or even the one wronged, but for you — that you would realize and act upon the deep, deep ties between us before God. That's what happened — and we felt just great.

13 And then, when we saw how Titus felt — his exuberance over your response — our joy doubled. It was wonderful to see how revived and refreshed he was by everything you did.

LIVE

Since we are spirits in bodies, tangible objects or physical activities can help us enter into prayer. If it's daytime, close the curtains or go into a room without windows. Light a candle and spend a few minutes watching the flame before you read and pray today. Let your awareness of the flame quiet your tendency to be aware only of yourself.

READ

Read the passage twice. According to Paul, what are God's reasons for using jarring things to bring us to repentance? How does Paul describe a life that's been turned around and brought back closer to God?

THINK

Now set the text aside and take a few moments to sit with your eyes closed and recall recent experiences you've had with sin. Did you repent? If so, how did God lead you to that? Did you resist? What turned you around? If you didn't repent, do you notice ways that God was reaching out to you that you refused? What were the thoughts that held you back?

PRAY

Go back to the passage again. Prayerfully reread Paul's perspective on repentance. How does his outlook interact with your current situation? Is there a message you sense God is speaking to you?

DAY 77

GOD ENCOUNTERS

On this seventh day, review and reflect on all you have read this week. Take the time to revel in the ways you've encountered God in the past six days.

GENEROUS OFFERINGS

2 CORINTHIANS 9:8-15

8-11 God can pour on the blessings in astonishing ways so that you're ready for anything and everything, more than just ready to do what needs to be done. As one psalmist puts it,

> He throws caution to the winds,
>   giving to the needy in reckless abandon.
> His right-living, right-giving ways
>   never run out, never wear out.

This most generous God who gives seed to the farmer that becomes bread for your meals is more than extravagant with you. He gives you something you can then give away, which grows into full-formed lives, robust in God, wealthy in every way, so that you can be generous in every way, producing with us great praise to God.

12-15 Carrying out this social relief work involves far more than helping meet the bare needs of poor Christians. It also produces abundant and bountiful thanksgivings to God. This relief offering is a prod to live at your very best, showing your gratitude to God by being openly obedient to the plain meaning of the Message of Christ. You show your gratitude through your generous offerings to your needy brothers and sisters, and really toward everyone. Meanwhile, moved by the extravagance of God in your lives, they'll respond by praying for you in passionate intercession for whatever you need. Thank God for this gift, his gift. No language can praise it enough!

READ

Read the passage, imagining that Paul is speaking these words specifically to you.

THINK

Paul talks here about generosity as an important element of God's character. Taking care of the poor is close to the heart of God. Jesus spoke — and lived — generously, just like his Father.

Do you think followers of God are known as being generous people? Why or why not?

In what ways can you grow in your generosity with your time? Your love? Your money? Your abilities? Your possessions? Your life?

PRAY

Walk around inside and outside your home. Look at your possessions: clothes, electronic equipment, books, furniture, paintings on the walls, maybe even the car in your driveway, and so on. What does all this stuff make you think? (Even if most of it belongs to others, like your parents, what's running through your head and heart?) Use Paul's words as the foundation for your communication with God, praying as you are walking around.

Talk with God about your desire to be more generous with the objects you possess. Ask him to bring to mind the people you could be more generous with today and in what way. Ask God to make you more like him — a person of generosity.

LIVE

Go and live with generosity at the forefront of your mind.

GOD'S HIDDEN SERVANTS

2 CORINTHIANS 11:21,23-30

21   I shouldn't admit it to you, but our stomachs aren't strong enough to tolerate that kind of stuff.

21,23   Since you admire the egomaniacs of the pulpit so much (remember, this is your old friend, the fool, talking), let me try my hand at it. . . . Are they servants of Christ? I can go them one better. (I can't believe I'm saying these things. It's crazy to talk this way! But I started, and I'm going to finish.)

23-27   I've worked much harder, been jailed more often, beaten up more times than I can count, and at death's door time after time. I've been flogged five times with the Jews' thirty-nine lashes, beaten by Roman rods three times, pummeled with rocks once. I've been shipwrecked three times, and immersed in the open sea for a night and a day. In hard traveling year in and year out, I've had to ford rivers, fend off robbers, struggle with friends, struggle with foes. I've been at risk in the city, at risk in the country, endangered by desert sun and sea storm, and betrayed by those I thought were my brothers. I've known drudgery and hard labor, many a long and lonely night without sleep, many a missed meal, blasted by the cold, naked to the weather.

28-29   And that's not the half of it, when you throw in the daily pressures and anxieties of all the churches. When someone gets to the end of his rope, I feel the desperation in my bones. When someone is duped into sin, an angry fire burns in my gut.

30   If I have to "brag" about myself, I'll brag about the humiliations that make me like Jesus.

READ

Read the passage aloud slowly, keeping in mind that the Corinthians were partial to slick preachers.

THINK

Which sort of teachers (of the Bible, of spiritual things) do you gravitate toward: the animated, joking, smooth servants of God or the hidden, suffering, unrecognized servants of God?

Paul was the second type. In those days, they didn't know him as we do — the great apostle Paul who wrote nearly half the New Testament. He may not have been all that popular a fellow.

Read the passage again silently. If you were to admire the apostle Paul, what in this passage describes what you would admire him for?

Keep in mind that Paul was also a person of joy. His joy was not in being well-known and appreciated. Instead he was one who encouraged his reader to "celebrate God all day, every day . . . *revel* in him!" (Philippians 4:4). When do you need Paul's sort of joy in your life?

PRAY

Ask God to give you discernment (not judgment) about his servants and which ones are best to follow. Ask God to give you great satisfaction in serving him regardless of how successful that service may look.

LIVE

Watch today for an opportunity to feel the desperation for another who is at the end of his or her rope, or to have an angry fire in your gut when someone is duped into sin. Make an effort to weep for those who weep and rejoice with those who rejoice.

RELATIONSHIPS ARE MESSY

2 CORINTHIANS 12:16-21

16-18   And why is it that I keep coming across these whiffs of gossip about how my self-support was a front behind which I worked an elaborate scam? Where's the evidence? Did I cheat or trick you through anyone I sent? I asked Titus to visit, and sent some brothers along. Did they swindle you out of anything? And haven't we always been just as aboveboard, just as honest?

19   I hope you don't think that all along we've been making our defense before you, the jury. You're not the jury; God is the jury — God revealed in Christ — and we make our case before him. And we've gone to all the trouble of supporting ourselves so that we won't be in the way or get in the way of your growing up.

20-21   I do admit that I have fears that when I come you'll disappoint me and I'll disappoint you, and in frustration with each other everything will fall to pieces — quarrels, jealousy, flaring tempers, taking sides, angry words, vicious rumors, swelled heads, and general bedlam. I don't look forward to a second humiliation by God among you, compounded by hot tears over that crowd that keeps sinning over and over in the same old ways, who refuse to turn away from the pigsty of evil, sexual disorder, and indecency in which they wallow.

READ

Read the passage aloud slowly.

THINK

Enter the scenes that Paul is describing. Envision the individual members of the Corinthian church he's writing to. Replay Paul's history with them — how he first came to the cosmopolitan city preaching the Message of Christ for the first time. Many believed and repented, and many formed new churches. Since then, those churches have helped support him financially, and he's acted as a spiritual mentor and father to them. Imagine what goes on in his mind as he anticipates visiting them again; think about what his last visit was like.

PRAY

Now read the passage again aloud. Notice the messiness of human relationships — misunderstandings, conflicts, and tensions. In the silence that follows your reading, consider your own relationships. Pick one in which you've felt the most recent tension or problems. Open up to God, asking him to show you what he wants you to know about it.

LIVE

Write down in a journal what God uncovered for you about your problematic relationship. Ask him to make clear anything he is asking you to notice or do about it, then sit quietly and attentively as you wait for his response. Don't assume that you should necessarily do anything; instead be open to how God leads you.

IN NEED OF CORRECTION

GALATIANS 1:6-12

6-9   I can't believe your fickleness — how easily you have turned traitor to him who called you by the grace of Christ by embracing a variant message! It is not a minor variation, you know; it is completely other, an alien message, a no-message, a lie about God. Those who are provoking this agitation among you are turning the Message of Christ on its head. Let me be blunt: If one of us — even if an angel from heaven! — were to preach something other than what we preached originally, let him be cursed. I said it once; I'll say it again: If anyone, regardless of reputation or credentials, preaches something other than what you received originally, let him be cursed.

10-12   Do you think I speak this strongly in order to manipulate crowds? Or curry favor with God? Or get popular applause? If my goal was popularity, I wouldn't bother being Christ's slave. Know this — I am most emphatic here, friends — this great Message I delivered to you is not mere human optimism. I didn't receive it through the traditions, and I wasn't taught it in some school. I got it straight from God, received the Message directly from Jesus Christ.

READ

Read the passage aloud. Reflect by writing your thoughts down in a journal or typing them into your computer.

THINK

This feels like a scathing lecture from Paul — and it certainly is. He is disgusted because the church in Galatia has turned from the true Message of the gospel to other slick teachers and optimistic (but empty) ways of thinking.

Consider carefully: What are the essentials of the gospel — the good news of Jesus Christ? What does it most certainly include? What does it most certainly not include?

Have you ever been tempted to turn from the Message of the gospel or to add to, delete, or alter portions of it to make it conveniently fit your life? Have you ever heard others add to, delete, or alter the Message of the gospel? What might be done about that? What are the consequences of doing such a thing?

What might Paul say to you if he were here today?

PRAY

Prayerfully reflect on the importance of the gospel Message. Ask God to give you a mind that discerns and carefully weighs the truth of the gospel and that knows how the gospel should be applied to your life.

LIVE

Spend a few minutes searching for and reading at least three key passages in your Bible that speak specifically to the meaning of the gospel.

NO LONGER TRYING TO BE GOOD

GALATIANS 2:16,19-21

16   We know very well that we are not set right with God by rule-keeping but only through personal faith in Jesus Christ. How do we know? We tried it — and we had the best system of rules the world has ever seen! Convinced that no human being can please God by self-improvement, we believed in Jesus as the Messiah so that we might be set right before God by trusting in the Messiah, not by trying to be good. . . .

19-21   What actually took place is this: I tried keeping rules and working my head off to please God, and it didn't work. So I quit being a "law man" so that I could be *God's* man. Christ's life showed me how, and enabled me to do it. I identified myself completely with him. Indeed, I have been crucified with Christ. My ego is no longer central. It is no longer important that I appear righteous before you or have your good opinion, and I am no longer driven to impress God. Christ lives in me. The life you see me living is not "mine," but it is lived by faith in the Son of God, who loved me and gave himself for me. I am not going to go back on that.

  Is it not clear to you that to go back to that old rule-keeping, peer-pleasing religion would be an abandonment of everything personal and free in my relationship with God? I refuse to do that, to repudiate God's grace. If a living relationship with God could come by rule-keeping, then Christ died unnecessarily.

READ

Read the passage aloud slowly.

THINK

Read it again silently.

1. What did Paul find that was better than trying to be good?
2. Which of the following astonishing statements by Paul do you find most intriguing? (The first three are truer the more the last two come to pass.)

   ☐ "My ego is no longer central."
   ☐ "It is no longer important that I appear righteous before you or have your good opinion."
   ☐ "I am no longer driven to impress God."
   ☐ "Christ lives in me."
   ☐ "The life you see me living is not 'mine,' but it is lived by faith in the Son of God."

   Read the passage one more time — very slowly — letting it sink into the innermost parts of you.

PRAY

Talk to God about Paul's amazing statements. Which of them do you want help in making true of yourself? To what degree do you really believe that "Christ lives in [you]"? If you need help believing this, tell God.

LIVE

Take something with you through your day to remind yourself that the life you now live is not yours, but is Christ's life in you. The item could be a cross, a piece of paper with this statement written on it, a stone on which you have written *LIFE*, or whatever will help remind you.

GROWTH: A RESULT OF HOW HARD YOU TRY?

GALATIANS 3:2-6

2-4   Let me put this question to you: How did your new life begin? Was it by working your heads off to please God? Or was it by responding to God's Message to you? Are you going to continue this craziness? For only crazy people would think they could complete by their own efforts what was begun by God. If you weren't smart enough or strong enough to begin it, how do you suppose you could perfect it? Did you go through this whole painful learning process for nothing? It is not yet a total loss, but it certainly will be if you keep this up!

5-6   Answer this question: Does the God who lavishly provides you with his own presence, his Holy Spirit, working things in your lives you could never do for yourselves, does he do these things because of your strenuous moral striving *or* because you trust him to do them in you? Don't these things happen among you just as they happened with Abraham? He believed God, and that act of belief was turned into a life that was right with God.

READ

As you read this passage, try not to identify yourself too firmly with the author's anger, but stay open to any similarities you recognize between yourself and his listeners.

THINK/PRAY

Pondering one question that particularly challenges you. For example, "Does God richly bless and change me because I try so hard to be good? Or because I trust him to do it?" Or ask yourself what "crazy" efforts you're making toward a transformational work that he's begun in you. Share your heart's response openly with the Father. Bring him your questions and concerns, and ask for his help in opening up to his model of growth.

LIVE

Take several minutes to try stepping outside your usual "craziness." Taste what it could be like to see growth as a process of letting God "complete . . . what was begun by God." Rest in the presence of his Holy Spirit, "lavishly provide[d to] you." Don't worry about how you'll grow spiritually; don't try to make a plan for how you'll change yourself. Use this time to practice simply being, finding out what it is to be yourself in the presence of Love.

DAY 84

GOD ENCOUNTERS

On this seventh day, review and reflect on all you have read this week. Take the time to revel in the ways you've encountered God in the past six days.

COMPLETE ACCESS TO THE INHERITANCE

GALATIANS 4:1-7

1-3 Let me show you the implications of this. As long as the heir is a minor, he has no advantage over the slave. Though legally he owns the entire inheritance, he is subject to tutors and administrators until whatever date the father has set for emancipation. That is the way it is with us: When we were minors, we were just like slaves ordered around by simple instructions (the tutors and administrators of this world), with no say in the conduct of our own lives.

4-7 But when the time arrived that was set by God the Father, God sent his Son, born among us of a woman, born under the conditions of the law so that he might redeem those of us who have been kidnapped by the law. Thus we have been set free to experience our rightful heritage. You can tell for sure that you are now fully adopted as his own children because God sent the Spirit of his Son into our lives crying out, "Papa! Father!" Doesn't that privilege of intimate conversation with God make it plain that you are not a slave, but a child? And if you are a child, you're also an heir, with complete access to the inheritance.

pty

READ

Read the passage at least five times. Take your time. Slow down and reflect on what you read.

THINK

Paul is a master craftsman of metaphors. And so we find him here in the middle of another word picture, contrasting the difference between the rights and privileges of a slave and those of an heir. We were once slaves, but as believers we are now called sons and daughters — heirs — and God desires for us to live in freedom, not slavery: "Thus we have been set free to experience our rightful heritage."

What does it mean for you to experience your rightful heritage in Christ? What does it mean to have freedom in your relationship with him? How do you temper that freedom so as not to abuse God's grace?

In what ways does being an heir rather than a slave change your interaction with your Father? Be specific.

PRAY

Imagine yourself in the lap of your Father, remembering that you have the "privilege of intimate conversation with God" and "complete access to the inheritance." With the mind-set of a child, pray like a child. Begin your prayer with "Papa." Pray freely and without fear, knowing that this childlike and intimate language is not only permissible but desirable. Tell him your fears. Tell him your joys. Tell him your dreams.

LIVE

Pray frequently, creatively, and confidently, knowing that you have great freedom to approach your heavenly Papa, who is always accessible to you.

GETTING OUR WAY

GALATIANS 5:16-17,19-23

16-17   My counsel is this: Live freely, animated and motivated by God's Spirit. Then you won't feed the compulsions of selfishness. For there is a root of sinful self-interest in us that is at odds with a free spirit, just as the free spirit is incompatible with selfishness. These two ways of life are anti-thetical, so that you cannot live at times one way and at times another way according to how you feel on any given day. . . .

19-21   It is obvious what kind of life develops out of trying to get your own way all the time: repetitive, loveless, cheap sex; a stinking accumulation of mental and emotional garbage; frenzied and joyless grabs for happiness; trinket gods; magic-show religion; paranoid loneliness; cutthroat competition; all-consuming-yet-never-satisfied wants; a brutal temper; an impotence to love or be loved; divided homes and divided lives; small-minded and lopsided pursuits; the vicious habit of depersonalizing everyone into a rival; uncontrolled and uncontrollable addictions; ugly parodies of community. I could go on.

    This isn't the first time I have warned you, you know. If you use your freedom this way, you will not inherit God's kingdom.

22-23   But what happens when we live God's way? He brings gifts into our lives, much the same way that fruit appears in an orchard — things like affection for others, exuberance about life, serenity. We develop a will-ingness to stick with things, a sense of compassion in the heart, and a conviction that a basic holiness permeates things and people. We find ourselves involved in loyal commitments, not needing to force our way in life, able to marshal and direct our energies wisely.

23   Legalism is helpless in bringing this about; it only gets in the way.

READ

Read the passage aloud slowly. Read verses 16-17 and 19-21 again slowly. What words or phrases stand out to you? Why do you think they stand out? Read verses 22-23 again slowly. What words or phrases stand out to you? Why do you think they stand out?

THINK

These two ways of life — self-focus and God-focus — negate each other. To live the first way shuts out the second. To live the second way shuts out the first. The first is empowered by the idea that we must get what we want when we want it. The second is empowered by a faithful, fruitful love for God.

PRAY

Talk to God about the ideas that stood out to you in verses 22-23. Tell God why these are attractive to you. Tell God how they reflect his deep character.

LIVE

Hold one of the following words in front of you today: *exuberance, serenity, willingness, compassion, conviction.* Let that word permeate what you do.

FREE FROM PLEASING OTHERS

GALATIANS 6:11-16

11-13 Now, in these last sentences, I want to emphasize in the bold scrawls of my personal handwriting the immense importance of what I have written to you. These people who are attempting to force the ways of circumcision on you have only one motive: They want an easy way to look good before others, lacking the courage to live by a faith that shares Christ's suffering and death. All their talk about the law is gas. They *themselves* don't keep the law! And they are highly selective in the laws they *do* observe. They only want you to be circumcised so they can boast of their success in recruiting you to their side. That is contemptible!

14-16 For my part, I am going to boast about nothing but the Cross of our Master, Jesus Christ. Because of that Cross, I have been crucified in relation to the world, set free from the stifling atmosphere of pleasing others and fitting into the little patterns that they dictate. Can't you see the central issue in all this? It is not what you and I do — submit to circumcision, reject circumcision. It is what *God* is doing, and he is creating something totally new, a free life! All who walk by this standard are the true Israel of God — his chosen people. Peace and mercy on them!

READ

Carefully read the passage.

THINK

This passage is rebuking first-century Christians for believing that ceremonial Jewish acts like circumcision could alleviate all guilt before God. Consider how you relate to this message. Who are you interested in impressing? How much energy do you expend figuring out ways to be more accepted by others? Is your security rooted in others, or is it rooted in your total acceptance by God?

Do you ever imagine God taking sides — either with you against the world or with everyone else against you? How would your life look if you lived to please only him?

PRAY

Let your thoughts lead you into conversation with God. Interact with him on what you're thinking about, remembering that he loves and accepts you. You might write things down as they come to mind, but don't let your writing shrink your awareness so you forget God's presence. Confide in him why you do what you do, even if you know your reasons are selfish or foolish.

LIVE

Return to the question of how your life would look if you lived only to please him — "to boast about nothing but the Cross of our Master." What one thing, even if tiny and internal, could you do to start living this way? Maybe you begin by asking God to give you a whiff of the air that exists beyond the "stifling atmosphere of pleasing others."

WHO WE ARE

EPHESIANS 1:11-19

11-12   It's in Christ that we find out who we are and what we are living for. Long before we first heard of Christ and got our hopes up, he had his eye on us, had designs on us for glorious living, part of the overall purpose he is working out in everything and everyone.

13-14   It's in Christ that you, once you heard the truth and believed it (this Message of your salvation), found yourselves home free — signed, sealed, and delivered by the Holy Spirit. This signet from God is the first install-ment on what's coming, a reminder that we'll get everything God has planned for us, a praising and glorious life.

15-19   That's why, when I heard of the solid trust you have in the Master Jesus and your outpouring of love to all the followers of Jesus, I couldn't stop thanking God for you — every time I prayed, I'd think of you and give thanks. But I do more than thank. I ask — ask the God of our Master, Jesus Christ, the God of glory — to make you intelligent and discerning in knowing him personally, your eyes focused and clear, so that you can see exactly what it is he is calling you to do, grasp the immensity of this glorious way of life he has for his followers, oh, the utter extravagance of his work in us who trust him — endless energy, boundless strength!

THINK

Consider your identity. Who are you — *really*? In what do you find your true identity and sense of worth? In other words, what makes you, you? Are the sources of your self-worth healthy or unhealthy? Jot down a few notes about how you see your identity.

READ

Read the passage silently, but mouth the words of the verses as you read. What does this passage say about your identity? What is Christ's role in shaping your identity? Refer to your notes. How does this picture of your identity compare to those initial thoughts?

PRAY

Paul includes several elements in his prayers for the church at Ephesus. It is full of thanksgiving, petitions for intimacy with the Father, clarity for direction, knowledge of a life lived with Christ, and strength.

Make Paul's prayer in verses 15-19 your own. For example, *I ask you — the God of my Master, Jesus Christ, the God of glory — to make me intelligent and discerning in knowing you personally.* And so on.

Next, ask God to bring to mind an individual who needs prayer. Come before God and pray these verses for that person's current situation and overall life. Pray for his or her identity. Make your prayer specific by replacing the applicable words in today's passage with the individual's name.

Are there others for whom you could pray this prayer? Spend time interceding for them as well.

LIVE

If the Spirit nudges you to do so, tell the person that you prayed specifically for him or her. Read that person the prayer from Scripture.

REALLY ALIVE IN CHRIST

EPHESIANS 2:1-6

1-6   It wasn't so long ago that you were mired in that old stagnant life of sin. You let the world, which doesn't know the first thing about living, tell you how to live. You filled your lungs with polluted unbelief, and then exhaled disobedience. We all did it, all of us doing what we felt like doing, when we felt like doing it, all of us in the same boat. It's a wonder God didn't lose his temper and do away with the whole lot of us. Instead, immense in mercy and with an incredible love, he embraced us. He took our sin-dead lives and made us alive in Christ. He did all this on his own, with no help from us! Then he picked us up and set us down in highest heaven in company with Jesus, our Messiah.

READ

Read the passage aloud slowly.

THINK

Read the passage again, noting the "old stagnant life" as described in the first part of the paragraph and all that God has done in the second part.

1. How do you relate to the "old stagnant life" described in verses 1-3?
2. How difficult or easy is it for you to believe that the "old stagnant life" is not in sync with "the first thing about living"?
3. Repeat in your own words what God has done in verses 4-6. What does this tell you about what God is really like?
4. How difficult or easy is it for you to believe that God is like that?

PRAY

Ask God to help you more easily believe in the goodness of life with him (verses 1-3) and in the goodness of God's own self (verses 4-6). Respond to God about what it's like to be surrounded by such goodness.

LIVE

Be aware of having an interactive life with this God who is unendingly compassionate and who makes us really alive all day long.

CHRIST'S EXTRAVAGANT LOVE

EPHESIANS 3:10-20

10 Through followers of Jesus like yourselves gathered in churches, this extraordinary plan of God is becoming known and talked about even among the angels!

11-13 All this is proceeding along lines planned all along by God and then executed in Christ Jesus. When we trust in him, we're free to say whatever needs to be said, bold to go wherever we need to go. So don't let my present trouble on your behalf get you down. Be proud!

14-19 My response is to get down on my knees before the Father, this magnificent Father who parcels out all heaven and earth. I ask him to strengthen you by his Spirit — not a brute strength but a glorious inner strength — that Christ will live in you as you open the door and invite him in. And I ask him that with both feet planted firmly on love, you'll be able to take in with all followers of Jesus the extravagant dimensions of Christ's love. Reach out and experience the breadth! Test its length! Plumb the depths! Rise to the heights! Live full lives, full in the fullness of God.

20 God can do anything, you know — far more than you could ever imagine or guess or request in your wildest dreams! He does it not by pushing us around but by working within us, his Spirit deeply and gently within us.

READ

As you read this passage, look for a word or theme that refreshes you. Maybe this will be Paul's specific description of God's "magnificent" strength and power, or the picture of being "free to say whatever needs to be said, bold to go wherever we need to go."

THINK/PRAY

Think about the portion of the passage you chose. Why do you think it touches you today? Are you feeling tired? Trapped? Discouraged?

Now sit in silence, picturing yourself opening the door to Christ and letting him come inside to be with you in your troubles. Talk to him about what is bringing you down.

Look back at the passage, and read—a few times, slowly—the part that spoke to you. What message does Christ want you to hear today? Savor this message and let it speak to your need.

LIVE

Pick a word from the passage that symbolizes what uplifted you. Write it down or doodle a picture that represents its meaning to you. Now put it where you will often see it and reflect on it. Maybe you'll use a sticky note and put it on your steering wheel, your bathroom mirror, or your microwave door. When you see it throughout the day, pause to recall Christ's Message to you.

DAY 91

GOD ENCOUNTERS

On this seventh day, review and reflect on all you have read this week. Take the time to revel in the ways you've encountered God in the past six days.

PERMEATED WITH ONENESS

EPHESIANS 4:1-6

1-3 In light of all this, here's what I want you to do. While I'm locked up here, a prisoner for the Master, I want you to get out there and walk — better yet, run! — on the road God called you to travel. I don't want any of you sitting around on your hands. I don't want anyone strolling off, down some path that goes nowhere. And mark that you do this with humility and discipline — not in fits and starts, but steadily, pouring yourselves out for each other in acts of love, alert at noticing differences and quick at mending fences.

4-6 You were all called to travel on the same road and in the same direction, so stay together, both outwardly and inwardly. You have one Master, one faith, one baptism, one God and Father of all, who rules over all, works through all, and is present in all. Everything you are and think and do is permeated with Oneness.

READ

Read this passage with another believer, if possible.

THINK

If you can, take this book to a spot within viewing distance of a road (whether busy or seldom traveled). Consider the road. Watch the cars and people that pass by.

Now think about the metaphor of traveling on a road used in this passage. Ponder Paul's words: "You were all called to travel on the same road and in the same direction, so stay together, both outwardly and inwardly." What does inward unity look like? What does outward unity look like? Do you know other followers of Christ who are not traveling on the same road or in the same direction you are?

"Everything you are and think and do is permeated with Oneness." Does this describe your relationships? Your church community? The body of Christ around the world? What can be done to strengthen this oneness with other believers?

With another believer (or several), brainstorm ways — little and big — to help create greater oneness in Christ.

PRAY

When you drive on or walk beside roads today, use that as a trigger to pray for unity among other believers — in your personal circles, in your town, and around the world.

LIVE

Do what you can to live in unity with others.

DRINKING THE SPIRIT OF GOD

EPHESIANS 5:15-20

15-16 So watch your step. Use your head. Make the most of every chance you get. These are desperate times!

17 Don't live carelessly, unthinkingly. Make sure you understand what the Master wants.

18-20 Don't drink too much wine. That cheapens your life. Drink the Spirit of God, huge draughts of him. Sing hymns instead of drinking songs! Sing songs from your heart to Christ. Sing praises over everything, any excuse for a song to God the Father in the name of our Master, Jesus Christ.

READ

Read the passage aloud slowly.

THINK

Read the passage again, picturing yourself in the crowd of people listening to this letter read aloud (as was done in those days). The writer, Paul, spent two years with your group and knows you well.

1. What does "live carelessly" mean to you?
2. How would you go about "drink[ing] the Spirit of God"? What would that look like for you?

Read the passage again and notice what words or phrases stand out to you. Why do you think they speak to you that way?

PRAY

Speak back to God the words that spoke to you. Tell God what they mean to you and what you would like to do about them. Talk to God about how well he knows you, that he would speak to you so personally.

LIVE

Each time you drink a liquid today, pause and picture yourself being filled with the liquid Spirit of God. Enjoy that.

RELATIONSHIPS FOR LIVING WELL

EPHESIANS 6:1-9

1-3   Children, do what your parents tell you. This is only right. "Honor your father and mother" is the first commandment that has a promise attached to it, namely, "so you will live well and have a long life."

4   Fathers, don't exasperate your children by coming down hard on them. Take them by the hand and lead them in the way of the Master.

5-8   Servants, respectfully obey your earthly masters but always with an eye to obeying the *real* master, Christ. Don't just do what you have to do to get by, but work heartily, as Christ's servants doing what God wants you to do. And work with a smile on your face, always keeping in mind that no matter who happens to be giving the orders, you're really serving God. Good work will get you good pay from the Master, regardless of whether you are slave or free.

9   Masters, it's the same with you. No abuse, please, and no threats. You and your servants are both under the same Master in heaven. He makes no distinction between you and them.

READ

Read the passage, letting it call to mind the relevant relationships in your life.

THINK

Mull over what this passage is saying about whole and healthy relationships — children to parents, fathers to children, and employees to employers. What is your reaction to the description given of each relationship? Perhaps you feel longing or maybe sadness or annoyance? Explore your reaction.

PRAY

Pick one relationship this passage brought to mind and take a few minutes to observe what kind of child, parent, employee, or student you are. How does your fulfillment of this role compare to the standard Paul sets? Ponder the models in your life for that role. How were you parented? How do your role models relate to their employers? Talk to Jesus about this, and share with him any disappointment, gratitude, or frustration you feel about your own role and your role models.

LIVE

What is Jesus' invitation to you in the relationship you selected? Perhaps it is just to continue growing in your awareness of what kind of person you are in relationships. Or perhaps you sense Jesus leading you toward a specific action. Make a note of what you hear so you can refer to it.

THE POSTURE OF GRATEFULNESS

PHILIPPIANS 1:3-6

3-6 Every time you cross my mind, I break out in exclamations of thanks to God. Each exclamation is a trigger to prayer. I find myself praying for you with a glad heart. I am so pleased that you have continued on in this with us, believing and proclaiming God's Message, from the day you heard it right up to the present. There has never been the slightest doubt in my mind that the God who started this great work in you would keep at it and bring it to a flourishing finish on the very day Christ Jesus appears.

READ

Read the passage. After doing so, write out the entire passage. Then read it again.

THINK

The subject of thankfulness in prayer will come up many times in this devotional, but there's no way to offer too much gratitude when we communicate with God. Of course it seems to be in our nature to approach God only when times are tough, when we feel like venting, or when we have a need. God listens to all our prayers, but it's hard to pray heartfelt, God-honoring prayers with an ungrateful and complaining spirit. We should *always* be grateful for *something* in prayer.

Paul models a thankful heart for us here as he reflects on the church in Philippi. On a scale of one to ten—one being "frequently ungrateful" and ten being "always thankful"—what number would you give your prayers? What number would your friends give your prayers? What would it take for your prayers to move toward ten?

LIVE/PRAY

Find a small photo of an old friend or family member. Place it in a location where you will see it often. Every time you look at the photo, pause and thank God for who that person is, what that person means to you, and who God is forming that person to become. Be reminded that God, who started this great work in him or her, will "keep at it and bring it to a flourishing finish" one day.

SETTING ASIDE ADVANTAGES

PHILIPPIANS 2:2-11

2-4   Agree with each other, love each other, be deep-spirited friends. Don't push your way to the front; don't sweet-talk your way to the top. Put yourself aside, and help others get ahead. Don't be obsessed with getting your own advantage. Forget yourselves long enough to lend a helping hand.

5-8   Think of yourselves the way Christ Jesus thought of himself. He had equal status with God but didn't think so much of himself that he had to cling to the advantages of that status no matter what. Not at all. When the time came, he set aside the privileges of deity and took on the status of a slave, became *human*! Having become human, he stayed human. It was an incredibly humbling process. He didn't claim special privileges. Instead, he lived a selfless, obedient life and then died a selfless, obedient death — and the worst kind of death at that — a crucifixion.

9-11   Because of that obedience, God lifted him high and honored him far beyond anyone or anything, ever, so that all created beings in heaven and on earth — even those long ago dead and buried — will bow in worship before this Jesus Christ, and call out in praise that he is the Master of all, to the glorious honor of God the Father.

READ

Read the passage aloud slowly, noticing the recurring words, such as *advantage, privileges, selfless, obedient, obedience.*

THINK

1. Read verses 5-8 again and consider what amazes you about Jesus, perhaps that he:

   - "didn't think so much of himself"
   - "[didn't] cling to the advantages"
   - "set aside the privileges"
   - "took on the status of a slave"
   - "lived a selfless, obedient life and then died a selfless, obedient death"

2. Read verses 9-11 again and consider what amazes you about God, perhaps that he:

   - "lifted [Jesus] high and honored him" more than any other (including God himself)
   - is honored by how people bow to worship Jesus Christ

3. Now read verses 2-4 again and consider what God is calling you to be or do.

4. In what way does your admiration for Jesus' and God's radical behavior (verses 5-11) inspire you to the behavior described in verses 2-4?

PRAY

Tell Jesus what you admire about his willingness to come to earth and his way of being while here. Tell God what you admire about his humility. Ask them to help you do whatever came to you in question 3.

LIVE

Look for opportunities today to help someone get ahead. If and when you do, sense Jesus' companionship in your efforts.

NOTHING LESS THAN TOTAL COMMITMENT

PHILIPPIANS 3:15-21

15-16 So let's keep focused on that goal, those of us who want everything God has for us. If any of you have something else in mind, something less than total commitment, God will clear your blurred vision — you'll see it yet! Now that we're on the right track, let's stay on it.

17-19 Stick with me, friends. Keep track of those you see running this same course, headed for this same goal. There are many out there taking other paths, choosing other goals, and trying to get you to go along with them. I've warned you of them many times; sadly, I'm having to do it again. All they want is easy street. They hate Christ's Cross. But easy street is a dead-end street. Those who live there make their bellies their gods; belches are their praise; all they can think of is their appetites.

20-21 But there's far more to life for us. We're citizens of high heaven! We're waiting the arrival of the Savior, the Master, Jesus Christ, who will transform our earthy bodies into glorious bodies like his own. He'll make us beautiful and whole with the same powerful skill by which he is putting everything as it should be, under and around him.

READ

Read the passage two times slowly.

THINK

Read again what Paul says about "total commitment." Write down honestly what you feel and think about it, without judging your own reaction.

Now read again what Paul says about those who are "choosing other goals" in life rather than knowing Jesus. What thoughts, memories, or feelings do you have as you read this? Jot them down.

Finally, read again, paying special attention to what Christians have to look forward to. What does this make you feel? Note the promise that evokes the greatest response in you.

LIVE

Think about a circumstance in your life that frustrates you with its monotony or pointlessness. Once again become aware of the goal in this passage: a simple and trusting openness to God and total commitment to what he has for you.

Now consider the following statement by Oswald Chambers: "The spiritual saint never believes circumstances to be haphazard, or thinks of his life as secular and sacred; he sees everything he is dumped down in as the means of securing the knowledge of Jesus Christ."[9] Do you believe that the God who intends to make you "beautiful and whole" is the same God who has allowed your circumstance? Why or why not?

PRAY

Ask Jesus to help you become totally committed to wanting "everything God has for [you]." Ask him to help you recognize and avoid "taking other paths, choosing other goals." Thank him that "there's far more to life for [you]."

DAY 98

GOD ENCOUNTERS

On this seventh day, review and reflect on all you have read this week. Take the time to revel in the ways you've encountered God in the past six days.

SHAPING WORRIES INTO PRAYERS

PHILIPPIANS 4:6-9

6-7 Don't fret or worry. Instead of worrying, pray. Let petitions and praises shape your worries into prayers, letting God know your concerns. Before you know it, a sense of God's wholeness, everything coming together for good, will come and settle you down. It's wonderful what happens when Christ displaces worry at the center of your life.

8-9 Summing it all up, friends, I'd say you'll do best by filling your minds and meditating on things true, noble, reputable, authentic, compelling, gracious — the best, not the worst; the beautiful, not the ugly; things to praise, not things to curse. Put into practice what you learned from me, what you heard and saw and realized. Do that, and God, who makes everything work together, will work you into his most excellent harmonies.

READ

Read the passage, including the expanded passage, if possible.

THINK

How do you handle something that worries you? Do you ignore the problem so you can put off thinking about it for as long as possible? Do you feel depressed and pessimistic about it, pretty sure of negative results, no matter what? Do you spend a lot of energy identifying a solution and working toward it? Whatever your answer, pinpoint your primary way of reacting. See if you know why you handle worry the way you do.

Now consider one worry you have today and how you've been dealing (or not dealing) with it.

PRAY

Sit in silence for a few minutes with your eyes closed. Breathe deeply and let your mind quiet down. Become aware of God's presence.

Express to God your concern. Even though he knows the situation, tell him all about it, every detail. In what way has your anxiety affected other areas of your life, such as relationships, work, or school? What's the worst-case scenario you're afraid might happen? Whether rational or irrational, share with God what you fear.

LIVE

Recall the Person you've experienced God to be in the past weeks and months. Reflect on previous notes you've made about experiencing God through his Message and prayer. From that, focus on three of his attributes. How do these elements of his character relate to your situation? What do they indicate about his presence with you right now? Picture this God in your mind. Remember today that this is the God who has heard your concern, the God who "will work you into his most excellent harmonies."

HE IS SUPREME

COLOSSIANS 1:15-23

15-18 We look at this Son and see the God who cannot be seen. We look at this Son and see God's original purpose in everything created. For everything, absolutely everything, above and below, visible and invisible, rank after rank after rank of angels — *everything* got started in him and finds its purpose in him. He was there before any of it came into existence and holds it all together right up to this moment. And when it comes to the church, he organizes and holds it together, like a head does a body.

18-20 He was supreme in the beginning and — leading the resurrection parade — he is supreme in the end. From beginning to end he's there, towering far above everything, everyone. So spacious is he, so roomy, that everything of God finds its proper place in him without crowding. Not only that, but all the broken and dislocated pieces of the universe — people and things, animals and atoms — get properly fixed and fit together in vibrant harmonies, all because of his death, his blood that poured down from the cross.

21-23 You yourselves are a case study of what he does. At one time you all had your backs turned to God, thinking rebellious thoughts of him, giving him trouble every chance you got. But now, by giving himself completely at the Cross, actually *dying* for you, Christ brought you over to God's side and put your lives together, whole and holy in his presence. You don't walk away from a gift like that! You stay grounded and steady in that bond of trust, constantly tuned in to the Message, careful not to be distracted or diverted. There is no other Message — just this one. Every creature under heaven gets this same Message. I, Paul, am a messenger of this Message.

READ

Wherever you are, stand up and read the passage aloud. Stand prayerfully in a posture that communicates to God respect and receptivity to his Word.

THINK

This passage speaks of the supremacy and power of God manifested through Jesus Christ. What specific attribute or characteristic of Jesus sticks out to you most in this passage? Why do you think it does?

"We look at this Son and see the God who cannot be seen. We look at this Son and see God's original purpose in everything created." What are specific, practical ways in which you can "look at this Son"?

What does the following mean? "He was supreme in the beginning and — leading the resurrection parade — he is supreme in the end." What implications does this have in your life today? Wonder about the supremacy of Christ.

PRAY

Reflect on the attribute of Christ that struck you (for example, maybe it was that everything "finds its purpose in him"). In what ways would the world be different if Christ did not possess that attribute? In what ways would your life be different? How and why?

LIVE

Live your day knowing that you serve — and are loved by — the God who holds the entire world together!

ALL-PURPOSE GARMENT

COLOSSIANS 3:3-5,12-17

3-4 Your old life is dead. Your new life, which is your *real* life — even though invisible to spectators — is with Christ in God. *He* is your life. When Christ (your real life, remember) shows up again on this earth, you'll show up, too — the real you, the glorious you. Meanwhile, be content with obscurity, like Christ.

5 And that means killing off everything connected with that way of death: sexual promiscuity, impurity, lust, doing whatever you feel like whenever you feel like it, and grabbing whatever attracts your fancy. That's a life shaped by things and feelings instead of by God. . . .

12-14 So, chosen by God for this new life of love, dress in the wardrobe God picked out for you: compassion, kindness, humility, quiet strength, discipline. Be even-tempered, content with second place, quick to forgive an offense. Forgive as quickly and completely as the Master forgave you. And regardless of what else you put on, wear love. It's your basic, all-purpose garment. Never be without it.

15-17 Let the peace of Christ keep you in tune with each other, in step with each other. None of this going off and doing your own thing. And cultivate thankfulness. Let the Word of Christ — the Message — have the run of the house. Give it plenty of room in your lives. Instruct and direct one another using good common sense. And sing, sing your hearts out to God! Let every detail in your lives — words, actions, whatever — be done in the name of the Master, Jesus, thanking God the Father every step of the way.

READ

Read the passage aloud slowly.

THINK

Read the passage again and consider these segments included in the process of stepping into the new life.

1. A new life is possible (verses 3-4).
2. We get rid of the old life (verse 5).
3. We put on the new life (verses 12-14).
4. We consider background thoughts and behavior needed to put on new life (verses 15-17).

Which segment of this process speaks to you most right now? Reread the verses that correspond to that segment. Now, what word or phrase in that segment speaks to you? Why do you think that is? How does that idea relate to the other segments? How does it relate to love, the "all-purpose garment"?

PRAY

Pray back to God the segment that speaks to you, personalizing it. For example, based on verse 15, *Please let the peace of Christ keep me in tune with others — show me that true peace of Christ!*

LIVE

Sit quietly in the idea that your old life really is dead. All the good, loving attitudes and behaviors of Jesus are open to you. Allow yourself to be invited to step into that today.

VIRTUE CHECKLIST

COLOSSIANS 4:2-6

2-4   Pray diligently. Stay alert, with your eyes wide open in gratitude. Don't forget to pray for us, that God will open doors for telling the mystery of Christ, even while I'm locked up in this jail. Pray that every time I open my mouth I'll be able to make Christ plain as day to them.

5-6   Use your heads as you live and work among outsiders. Don't miss a trick. Make the most of every opportunity. Be gracious in your speech. The goal is to bring out the best in others in a conversation, not put them down, not cut them out.

READ

Read this passage several times, each time narrowing your focus to the part that challenges you the most.

THINK

What did you focus on? Was it a virtuous action that is not part of your lifestyle? Or perhaps it was something you already do, but you noticed something different about the way or reason why Paul says to do it. What is your emotional response when you think of changing this area of your life? Do you feel eager? Overwhelmed? Threatened or protective? Unsure?

PRAY

Talk with Jesus about the item on Paul's list of virtues that challenged you most and about how you responded to it. Sit in silence to wait for what Jesus might have to say to you.

LIVE

As you read the following statement made by Saint Bernard of Clairvaux, also consider what Paul tells Christians to do in today's passage: "If then you are wise, you will show yourself rather as a reservoir than as a canal. For a canal spreads abroad water as it receives it, but a reservoir waits until it is filled before overflowing, and thus communicates, without loss to itself, its superabundant water. In the Church at the present day, we have many canals, few reservoirs."[10]

Are you more like a canal, a reservoir, or something else altogether? Would others who know you agree? Talk with Jesus about this and be open to what he is showing you about yourself. In what way is he inviting you to live differently?

ONLY GOD APPROVAL

1 THESSALONIANS 2:3-8

3-5 God tested us thoroughly to make sure we were qualified to be trusted with this Message. Be assured that when we speak to you we're not after crowd approval—only God approval. Since we've been put through that battery of tests, you're guaranteed that both we and the Message are free of error, mixed motives, or hidden agendas. We never used words to butter you up. No one knows that better than you. And God knows we never used words as a smoke screen to take advantage of you.

6-8 Even though we had some standing as Christ's apostles, we never threw our weight around or tried to come across as important, with you or anyone else. We weren't aloof with you. We took you just as you were. We were never patronizing, never condescending, but we cared for you the way a mother cares for her children. We loved you dearly. Not content to just pass on the Message, we wanted to give you our hearts. And we *did*.

READ

Read the passage, noting the word *approval*.

THINK

It's tempting to promote ourselves, to see ourselves more highly than we ought. If we examine ourselves honestly, we will have to admit that we are often trying to win the approval of the crowd.

Think back over the past week. What decisions did you make solely to look good in the eyes of others? What would it take for you to go through today without making decisions based on trying to make yourself look good? What would it take for you to live today for "only God approval"?

PRAY

Confess those recent circumstances when you were tempted to seek approval from other people. Ask God to help you be "free of error, mixed motives, [and] hidden agendas." Ask him to help you focus your desire for acceptance and approval entirely on him.

LIVE

Before every decision, before every comment, ask yourself, *What is my motive? Is it to get approval from the crowd or to get approval from God?* Let these questions make you aware today of how — and why — you make decisions.

SOMEONE ELSE'S FAITH AND LOVE

1 THESSALONIANS 3:6-13

6-8   But now that Timothy is back, bringing this terrific report on your faith and love, we feel a lot better. It's especially gratifying to know that you continue to think well of us, and that you want to see us as much as we want to see you! In the middle of our trouble and hard times here, just knowing how you're doing keeps us going. Knowing that your faith is alive keeps us alive.

9-10   What would be an adequate thanksgiving to offer God for all the joy we experience before him because of you? We do what we can, praying away, night and day, asking for the bonus of seeing your faces again and doing what we can to help when your faith falters.

11-13   May God our Father himself and our Master Jesus clear the road to you! And may the Master pour on the love so it fills your lives and splashes over on everyone around you, just as it does from us to you. May you be infused with strength and purity, filled with confidence in the presence of God our Father when our Master Jesus arrives with all his followers.

READ

Read the passage aloud slowly.

THINK

Ask God to bring to mind those you know who live their lives before God routinely showing "faith and love" (a really alive faith) and giving others joy. You may not know these people well or see them often (they may be missionaries from your church, friends of friends, or speakers you've listened to), but the way they live reassures you that this kind of life is possible. Read the passage again in light of these people.

PRAY

First, thank God for these people, that:

- their faith and love make you feel better
- they think well of you and you want to see them
- their faith is so alive it keeps you more alive
- you experience joy because of them

Second, pray for these people who, although they may seem so mature, still need your prayers. Pray that:

- if their faith falters, someone (maybe you) can help them
- God the Father and Jesus the Master will clear their roads
- Jesus will pour into their lives a love that fills them and "splashes over on everyone"
- they may be "infused with strength and purity"
- they may be "filled with confidence in the presence of God"

LIVE

Rejoice restfully that people who love God and live the Message really do exist in this world.

DAY 105

GOD ENCOUNTERS

On this seventh day, review and reflect on all you have read this week. Take the time to revel in the ways you've encountered God in the past six days.

NOT A SET-UP FOR REJECTION

1 THESSALONIANS 5:1-10

1-3   I don't think, friends, that I need to deal with the question of when all this is going to happen. You know as well as I that the day of the Master's coming can't be posted on our calendars. He won't call ahead and make an appointment any more than a burglar would. About the time everybody's walking around complacently, congratulating each other — "We've sure got it made! Now we can take it easy!" — suddenly everything will fall apart. It's going to come as suddenly and inescapably as birth pangs to a pregnant woman.

4-8   But friends, you're not in the dark, so how could you be taken off guard by any of this? You're sons of Light, daughters of Day. We live under wide open skies and know where we stand. So let's not sleepwalk through life like those others. Let's keep our eyes open and be smart. People sleep at night and get drunk at night. But not us! Since we're creatures of Day, let's act like it. Walk out into the daylight sober, dressed up in faith, love, and the hope of salvation.

9-10   God didn't set us up for an angry rejection but for salvation by our Master, Jesus Christ. He died for us, a death that triggered life. Whether we're awake with the living or asleep with the dead, we're *alive* with him!

READ

Read the passage twice.

THINK

When you think about the end of the world and Jesus' return to Earth, what do you feel? Nervous? Excited? Halfhearted interest? In everyday life, how often do you think, feel, act, or plan as though you really believe that Jesus will come back someday soon?

PRAY

Prayerfully think about Paul's statement: "We . . . know where we stand." What does it stir up in you? Do you feel confident or uncertain about where you stand with Jesus? Talk to him about your reaction to this phrase.

LIVE

Ruth Haley Barton voices the questions "Is God really good? If I trust myself to him, isn't there a good chance that I will wind up where I least want to be or that God will withhold what I want the most? Isn't God a little bit like Lucy in the Peanuts comic strip, who pulls the football away just as Charlie Brown gives himself completely to the kick, causing him to fall flat on his face?"[11]

Take a moment to absorb these questions and reconsider Paul's statement that "God didn't set us up for an angry rejection but for salvation." How do your deep-down-inside expectations of God correspond with Paul's perspective? With the perspective Barton describes? Share with God your honest beliefs about him and your expectations of how he'll treat you.

Suspend for a few minutes whatever disbelief you have, and imagine you truly believe God is trustworthy. How might you live differently?

WE GIVE THANKS

2 THESSALONIANS 1:3-4

3-4   You need to know, friends, that thanking God over and over for you is not only a pleasure; it's a must. We *have* to do it. Your faith is growing phenomenally; your love for each other is developing wonderfully. Why, it's only right that we give thanks. We're so proud of you; you're so steady and determined in your faith despite all the hard times that have come down on you. We tell everyone we meet in the churches all about you.

READ

Read this passage very slowly and cautiously. Imagine yourself as a surgeon carefully cutting and dissecting it. Give focused attention to each word.

THINK/PRAY

What or whom are you grateful for today? Why? Pause and give thanks to God for these now.

Who is growing in their faith, maturing into God's likeness, and loving others well? Thank God for them now, including names and details.

Who needs to grow more in their faith, needs to mature further into God's likeness, and could love others more appropriately and generously? Thank God for them and pray for them now, including names and details.

Which followers of Christ have fallen on hard times but are determined and are persevering? Thank God for them and pray for them now, including names and details. Pray also for the persecuted church — those Christ-followers around the globe who are being arrested and tortured and murdered simply because of what they believe. Thank God for their incredible passion and commitment to Jesus. Finally, ask God to give you the same courage, commitment, and love for Christ.

LIVE

Carry all these individuals in your thoughts today. Ask God to bring them to mind during the coming week. As you remember them, "thanking God over and over," pray for them.

LIFE IN THE SPIRIT

2 THESSALONIANS 2:13-17

13-14　Meanwhile, we've got our hands full continually thanking God for you, our good friends — so loved by God! God picked you out as his from the very start. Think of it: included in God's original plan of salvation by the bond of faith in the living truth. This is the life of the Spirit he invited you to through the Message we delivered, in which you get in on the glory of our Master, Jesus Christ.

15-17　So, friends, take a firm stand, feet on the ground and head high. Keep a tight grip on what you were taught, whether in personal conversation or by our letter. May Jesus himself and God our Father, who reached out in love and surprised you with gifts of unending help and confidence, put a fresh heart in you, invigorate your work, enliven your speech.

READ

Read the passage aloud slowly. Then recall the small, inconsequential things that have occupied your thoughts in the last few moments, hours, or days.

THINK

Read the passage again, noting how Paul viewed an average life as so spectacular because he was immersed in the Trinitarian reality (God, Jesus, and Holy Spirit in verses 13-14).

1. Which of these truths about God's unseen reality most captivate you?

   ☐ You are "so loved by God!"
   ☐ You have a "bond of faith in the living truth" with others.
   ☐ You're invited to life in the Spirit.
   ☐ "You get in on the glory of our Master, Jesus Christ."
   ☐ God reaches out to you in love.
   ☐ God surprises you "with gifts of unending help and confidence."
   ☐ God can "put a fresh heart in you."
   ☐ God can "invigorate your work."
   ☐ God can "enliven your speech."

2. Think about today's events — even mundane ones. Which of the truths mentioned in question 1 do you need to link with each event?

PRAY

Pray about each event, that you will live in this unseen reality, that you'll see how these truths are present. For example, pray about a conversation or a homework assignment or a work project, that you'll participate in it knowing you are loved and receiving God's gifts of unending help and confidence.

LIVE

Pick one of these truths about life in the Spirit and sense its reality. If you have trouble doing this, ask God to help you.

IF YOU DON'T WORK, YOU DON'T EAT

2 THESSALONIANS 3:6-15

6-9   Our orders — backed up by the Master, Jesus — are to refuse to have anything to do with those among you who are lazy and refuse to work the way we taught you. Don't permit them to freeload on the rest. We showed you how to pull your weight when we were with you, so get on with it. We didn't sit around on our hands expecting others to take care of us. In fact, we worked our fingers to the bone, up half the night moonlighting so you wouldn't be burdened with taking care of us. And it wasn't because we didn't have a right to your support; we did. We simply wanted to provide an example of diligence, hoping it would prove contagious.

10-13   Don't you remember the rule we had when we lived with you? "If you don't work, you don't eat." And now we're getting reports that a bunch of lazy good-for-nothings are taking advantage of you. This must not be tolerated. We command them to get to work immediately — no excuses, no arguments — and earn their own keep. Friends, don't slack off in doing your duty.

14-15   If anyone refuses to obey our clear command written in this letter, don't let him get by with it. Point out such a person and refuse to subsidize his freeloading. Maybe then he'll think twice. But don't treat him as an enemy. Sit him down and talk about the problem as someone who cares.

READ

Read the passage carefully.

THINK

Why do you think Paul is making such a big deal out of Christians who freeload off others? Why is he encouraging those in Thessalonica to make a big deal out of it? In what ways do you think laziness and freeloading impact relationships?

PRAY

Read the passage again, this time listening for a word or phrase that stands out to you, such as "duty," "excuses," or "[not] as an enemy . . . [but as] someone who cares." Chew on this for a few minutes. Share with God what pops up in you as you consider it.

Now read again the part of the passage that contains the word or phrase. Why do you think this word is standing out to you today? Does it trigger a fear? Does it challenge you? What part of your life does it touch?

LIVE

Read the whole passage one last time. This time, listen for the action or attitude God is inviting you to take on this week. Maybe he's asking you to lovingly sit down with a friend and speak plainly about her freeloading. Maybe he wants you to start looking for a job or to stop "borrowing" or using stuff that isn't yours. Make a note of how you can take steps in the direction God is indicating. If you are especially aware of God's presence with you when you take these steps, what might the impact be?

UNCONTAMINATED BY SELF-INTEREST

1 TIMOTHY 1:3-7

3-4 On my way to the province of Macedonia, I advised you to stay in Ephesus. Well, I haven't changed my mind. Stay right there on top of things so that the teaching stays on track. Apparently some people have been introducing fantasy stories and fanciful family trees that digress into silliness instead of pulling the people back into the center, deepening faith and obedience.

5-7 The whole point of what we're urging is simply *love* — love uncontaminated by self-interest and counterfeit faith, a life open to God. Those who fail to keep to this point soon wander off into cul-de-sacs of gossip. They set themselves up as experts on religious issues, but haven't the remotest idea of what they're holding forth with such imposing eloquence.

THINK

Paul as mentor has sent carefully written instructions to his disciple Timothy. This is the first volume of his guidance for Timothy, urging him as a young leader to mature in Christ. Among the complexities of life, Paul boils the message down to one simple concept: love. Not just love, but "love uncontaminated by self-interest and counterfeit faith, a life open to God."

READ

With this background in mind, meditate on the passage.

PRAY

While remaining open to God, consider what love looks like when it's "uncontaminated by self-interest and counterfeit faith." Then ask God the following questions, pausing between each one to listen to the Holy Spirit's response:

God, what about my love is contaminated by self-interest? Ask God to help remove the contamination of selfishness in your life.

Father, what about my love is counterfeit or fake? Ask for courage to be authentic with God, others, and yourself.

Lord, what about my life and love is closed off, hidden, or resistant to you and your purposes? Ask God to give you the willingness and to help you be more open to his purposes, even if doing so feels uncertain and scary.

LIVE

Go live and love selflessly, authentically, and openly.

HUMBLE CONTEMPLATION

1 TIMOTHY 2:1-2,8-9

1-2   The first thing I want you to do is pray. Pray every way you know how, for everyone you know. Pray especially for rulers and their governments to rule well so we can be quietly about our business of living simply, in humble contemplation. . . .

8-9   Since prayer is at the bottom of all this, what I want mostly is for men to pray — not shaking angry fists at enemies but raising holy hands to God. And I want women to get in there with the men in humility before God, not primping before a mirror or chasing the latest fashions.

READ

Read the passage aloud slowly.

THINK

Read the passage again, noting what is said about prayer:

- how to pray: "every way you know how" and "raising holy hands"
- government-related prayer: good ruling so through simple, humble, contemplative living, the Message about Christ may spread
- tone of prayer: "humble contemplation" and women praying in humility
- pray for: "everyone you know" and "rulers"
- outcome of prayer: the Message will spread, women will do "something beautiful for God" (verse 10)

Read the passage one more time. What do you think God is telling you about how you need to pray?

PRAY

Lift holy hands as you ask God to lead you in praying that governments will "rule well so [Christians] can be quietly about [their] business of living simply, in humble contemplation."

LIVE

Sit quietly with your hands raised, outstretched, eager for God's Message to permeate the nations of our planet.

DAY 112

GOD ENCOUNTERS

On this seventh day, review and reflect on all you have read this week. Take the time to revel in the ways you've encountered God in the past six days.

PRECONDITIONS OF LEADERSHIP

1 TIMOTHY 3:1-13

1-7　If anyone wants to provide leadership in the church, good! But there are preconditions: A leader must be well-thought-of, committed to his wife, cool and collected, accessible, and hospitable. He must know what he's talking about, not be overfond of wine, not pushy but gentle, not thin-skinned, not money-hungry. He must handle his own affairs well, attentive to his own children and having their respect. For if someone is unable to handle his own affairs, how can he take care of God's church? He must not be a new believer, lest the position go to his head and the Devil trip him up. Outsiders must think well of him, or else the Devil will figure out a way to lure him into his trap.

8-13　The same goes for those who want to be servants in the church: serious, not deceitful, not too free with the bottle, not in it for what they can get out of it. They must be reverent before the mystery of the faith, not using their position to try to run things. Let them prove themselves first. If they show they can do it, take them on. No exceptions are to be made for women — same qualifications: serious, dependable, not sharp-tongued, not overfond of wine. Servants in the church are to be committed to their spouses, attentive to their own children, and diligent in looking after their own affairs. Those who do this servant work will come to be highly respected, a real credit to this Jesus-faith.

READ

Read this passage a few times slowly and carefully.

THINK

As you absorb the moral expectations presented in this passage, what is your reaction? Perhaps you desire to change, or perhaps you feel irritated. Maybe you feel shame or guilt. Maybe relief. Does reading this make you want to be a leader? If not, why not? Share your reaction with God.

PRAY

Take several minutes to read the text again slowly, letting each instruction direct you toward a new area of your heart to examine with the Holy Spirit. (Don't feel that you must work your way through the entire passage: The goal is to uncover content for prayer, not get through the entire list.) In which areas does your life look different from the model Paul is describing? For example, you've been more pushy than gentle with someone, or you've been more unreliable than dependable. Tell God about what you find.

LIVE

Ask God to show you what it would look like to embrace transformation in an area you've examined today, realizing that starting with baby steps might be just right for you. Take courage that "our personalities are transformed — not lost — in the furnace of God's love."[12] God's transformation will not obliterate your personality; instead, the process will make you more into the one-of-a-kind you who God made you to be.

⊕ GET THE WORD OUT

1 TIMOTHY 4:10-16

10   This is why we've thrown ourselves into this venture so totally. We're banking on the living God, Savior of all men and women, especially believers.

11-14   Get the word out. Teach all these things. And don't let anyone put you down because you're young. Teach believers with your life: by word, by demeanor, by love, by faith, by integrity. Stay at your post reading Scripture, giving counsel, teaching. And that special gift of ministry you were given when the leaders of the church laid hands on you and prayed—keep that dusted off and in use.

15-16   Cultivate these things. Immerse yourself in them. The people will all see you mature right before their eyes! Keep a firm grasp on both your character and your teaching. Don't be diverted. Just keep at it. Both you and those who hear you will experience salvation.

READ

Read the passage, focusing on the words *teach* and *keep*.

THINK

In these verses, Paul, as almost a father figure, passes on wise words to young Timothy — and to us — about modeling our faith.

How can we be a part of that, no matter how old we are?

On a scale of one to ten — one being spiritual flabbiness and ten being spiritually fit — how would you rate your spiritual fitness? Why did you give yourself that rating?

How well are you "teach[ing] believers with your life" in these five areas: "by word, by demeanor, by love, by faith, by integrity"? Very well? In which areas? Not so well? In which areas? How can you make your life a better teacher in all of these?

PRAY

See if you can open your life to God like you would open a book. Consider the areas (such as school, family, work, and other activities), and write them down if that helps. Acknowledge to God your openness, then invite him to do his work in your life — whatever that might be — encouraging you, challenging you, and shaping your words, your demeanor, your love, your faith, and your integrity.

LIVE

Write these five words on an index card: *word, demeanor, love, faith, integrity.* Ask God to help you teach with your life in these specific areas throughout your day.

THE SPECIAL MINISTRY

1 TIMOTHY 5:1-4,7-10

1-2   Don't be harsh or impatient with an older man. Talk to him as you would your own father, and to the younger men as your brothers. Reverently honor an older woman as you would your mother, and the younger women as sisters.

3-4,7-8   Take care of widows who are destitute. If a widow has family members to take care of her, let them learn that religion begins at their own doorstep and that they should pay back with gratitude some of what they have received. This pleases God immensely. . . . Tell these things to the people so that they will do the right thing in their extended family. Anyone who neglects to care for family members in need repudiates the faith. That's worse than refusing to believe in the first place.

9-10   Sign some widows up for the special ministry of offering assistance. They will in turn receive support from the church. They must be over sixty, married only once, and have a reputation for helping out with children, strangers, tired Christians, the hurt and troubled.

READ

Read the passage aloud slowly.

THINK

Before reading the passage again, consider the following cultural ideas. Which ones have you unconsciously accepted?

- ☐ Older people and younger people don't mix much.
- ☐ Older people are retired, so they don't do "special ministry." (You don't know many people who help out "with children, strangers, tired Christians, the hurt and troubled.")
- ☐ Older people are tired and don't want to do much at church anymore.
- ☐ Older people aren't generally the people you go to for advice.
- ☐ Older people have Social Security benefits and don't need anyone's help.
- ☐ Older people are people you feel sorry for, not "reverently honor."

Read the passage again. Envision the sort of older person Paul was talking about. What older person do you know who is like the one Paul describes? In what small ways might you "reverently honor" this person? Try to wrap your mind around the idea that you can *look forward* to being such an older person.

PRAY

Thank God for older people in your life who resemble Paul's description. Pray for those who need more of what Paul describes. Pray for yourself that you'll be this sort of older person.

LIVE

Sit quietly. Pretend your joints don't work as well as they used to. Ponder what it would be like to still be eager to get up every day to be with Jesus and partner with him in what he's doing in the world.

BEING YOURSELF BEFORE GOD

1 TIMOTHY 6:6-12

6-8   A devout life does bring wealth, but it's the rich simplicity of being yourself before God. Since we entered the world penniless and will leave it penniless, if we have bread on the table and shoes on our feet, that's enough.

9-10   But if it's only money these leaders are after, they'll self-destruct in no time. Lust for money brings trouble and nothing but trouble. Going down that path, some lose their footing in the faith completely and live to regret it bitterly ever after.

11-12   But you, Timothy, man of God: Run for your life from all this. Pursue a righteous life — a life of wonder, faith, love, steadiness, courtesy. Run hard and fast in the faith. Seize the eternal life, the life you were called to, the life you so fervently embraced in the presence of so many witnesses.

READ

Read the passage twice.

THINK

Mull over Paul's advice to Timothy. Do you agree with his statements and assumptions about material wealth? About the value of being yourself before God? Why or why not? Explore your thoughts and share them with God.

PRAY

Consider your belongings, including favorite things and stuff you don't usually think about. In what ways might some of these items get in the way of you being yourself, plain and simple, before God? In what way does your attachment to these possessions alter your view of who you are? (Don't be too quick to answer here.)

LIVE

Read the passage again, considering more carefully Paul's description of "a righteous life." Do you notice an especially strong desire for any of these qualities? Listen for what God may be saying to you through the text and through your desire. Is he inviting you to do anything — even something small — in response to this time today?

RUN AFTER MATURE RIGHTEOUSNESS

2 TIMOTHY 2:22-26

22-26   Run away from infantile indulgence. Run after mature righteousness — faith, love, peace — joining those who are in honest and serious prayer before God. Refuse to get involved in inane discussions; they always end up in fights. God's servant must not be argumentative, but a gentle listener and a teacher who keeps cool, working firmly but patiently with those who refuse to obey. You never know how or when God might sober them up with a change of heart and a turning to the truth, enabling them to escape the Devil's trap, where they are caught and held captive, forced to run his errands.

READ

Slowly read these verses. Let their message saturate your heart and mind.

THINK

In Paul's second leadership letter to Timothy, he writes words of encouragement and challenge that we, too, need to take to heart in the coming week. Paul is talking about some aspects of a mature faith.

Imagine he is sitting beside you, speaking these words to you directly. How do you feel when you hear them? What part of the passage resonates most with you? Why? Maybe "infantile indulgence" seems a little patronizing. Perhaps "mature righteousness" seems impossible or defeating. Maybe with some people you've lost hope that "God might sober them up."

PRAY

Sit in a comfortable position, being silent and as still as you can. Ask God *why* he has given you this particular piece of instruction through Paul (the one that resonated most with you). Listen for the gentle whisper of God's voice in the midst of the silence. Maybe he will show you a spot of childishness or one of righteousness. Maybe he will offer you hope.

LIVE

As you continue to sit in silence, explore what God might want you to do with this piece of instruction. How are you to live it out today? This week? This month?

GOD-BREATHED AND USEFUL

2 TIMOTHY 3:1-5,15-17

1-5   Don't be naive. There are difficult times ahead. As the end approaches, people are going to be self-absorbed, money-hungry, self-promoting, stuck-up, profane, contemptuous of parents, crude, coarse, dog-eat-dog, unbending, slanderers, impulsively wild, savage, cynical, treacherous, ruthless, bloated windbags, addicted to lust, and allergic to God. They'll make a show of religion, but behind the scenes they're animals. Stay clear of these people. . . .

15-17   Why, you took in the sacred Scriptures with your mother's milk! There's nothing like the written Word of God for showing you the way to salvation through faith in Christ Jesus. Every part of Scripture is God-breathed and useful one way or another — showing us truth, exposing our rebellion, correcting our mistakes, training us to live God's way. Through the Word we are put together and shaped up for the tasks God has for us.

READ

Read the passage aloud slowly.

THINK

Before dismissing the first paragraph as a description of people other than yourself, consider that Western culture, in general (and our individual selves, in particular), tends to be self-absorbed, self-promoting, cynical, and addicted to lust.

Read the passage again. This time notice the enormous change from the first paragraph to the second.

1. How does the way Scripture moves us (verse 16) help us to be different from the general culture?
2. Scripture is God-breathed — words breathed to you from our relational God, not a bunch of rules. Picture God speaking to you, "showing [you] truth, exposing [y]our rebellion, correcting [y]our mistakes, training [you] to live [his] way."

Can you picture God doing these things in ways exactly right for you? In gentle yet firm ways? To rescue you before you blow it?

PRAY

Ask God to help you be open to his showing you truth, exposing your rebellion, correcting your mistakes, and training you to live his way. Ask him to show you specific details, if any, that you need to know at this moment.

LIVE

Imagine what living an interactive life with God would be like, one in which all day long you experience him gently showing you truth, exposing your rebellion, correcting your mistakes, and training you to live his way. Why would this be the best way to live?

DAY 119

GOD ENCOUNTERS

On this seventh day, review and reflect on all you have read this week. Take the time to revel in the ways you've encountered God in the past six days.

AN HONEST JUDGE

2 TIMOTHY 4:1-8

1-2   I can't impress this on you too strongly. God is looking over your shoulder. Christ himself is the Judge, with the final say on everyone, living and dead. He is about to break into the open with his rule, so proclaim the Message with intensity; keep on your watch. Challenge, warn, and urge your people. Don't ever quit. Just keep it simple.

3-5   You're going to find that there will be times when people will have no stomach for solid teaching, but will fill up on spiritual junk food — catchy opinions that tickle their fancy. They'll turn their backs on truth and chase mirages. But *you* — keep your eye on what you're doing; accept the hard times along with the good; keep the Message alive; do a thorough job as God's servant.

6-8   You take over. I'm about to die, my life an offering on God's altar. This is the only race worth running. I've run hard right to the finish, believed all the way. All that's left now is the shouting — God's applause! Depend on it, he's an honest judge. He'll do right not only by me, but by everyone eager for his coming.

READ

Read Paul's instructions to his apprentice Timothy, trying to identify the primary theme.

THINK

What common thread runs through all of Paul's statements and instructions here? Perhaps it's the tone of what he's saying (such as urgent or tender), or maybe it's that every statement somehow relates to a particular object or event (such as Christ's judgment of everyone, or people-pleasing versus God-pleasing). Write down the theme you see.

PRAY

Read the passage again with the theme in mind. Notice how each part of the passage unpacks the meaning even more. What especially stands out to you? Perhaps it's the reason that repentance and evangelism are so important or the anticipation of standing before God as he looks at your life. Think about what you discover, and be transparent with God about it.

LIVE

Now read the passage once more, this time listening for what you sense God, through the text, is saying to you personally. Maybe he's drawing your attention to your need to please people, or maybe you're relieved to understand more clearly that repentance isn't about being perfect (a mirage) but about living in accordance with reality. What will you do with what God is showing you? Sit in silence for a few minutes. Jot down your new intention.

AGENT OF CHRIST

TITUS 1:1-4

1-4   I, Paul, am God's slave and Christ's agent for promoting the faith among God's chosen people, getting out the accurate word on God and how to respond rightly to it. My aim is to raise hopes by pointing the way to life without end. This is the life God promised long ago — and he doesn't break promises! And then when the time was ripe, he went public with his truth. I've been entrusted to proclaim this Message by order of our Savior, God himself. Dear Titus, legitimate son in the faith: Receive everything God our Father and Jesus our Savior give you!

READ

Read the opening words of greeting from Paul to Titus in these verses.

THINK

Paul describes himself as "Christ's agent for promoting the faith among God's chosen people." Are you "God's slave and Christ's agent"? Do those terms accurately describe your life? Why or why not? How can your life be lived in such a way that you are "getting out the accurate word on God" to those around you? How can your life be "promoting the faith" among others by word and action? Take time to consider these questions, being specific.

Paul gives the purpose of his life to Titus by saying, "My aim is to raise hopes by pointing the way to life without end. This is the life God promised long ago — and he doesn't break promises!" In what way does God raise hopes? Has he raised your hopes?

PRAY

Ask Christ to help you be his agent. Invite him to reveal to you how you might best "respond rightly" to his Word.

LIVE

"Respond rightly" to what you hear from God, remembering that you go forth into this day as an agent of Christ.

A GOD-FILLED LIFE

TITUS 2:11-14

11-14 God's readiness to give and forgive is now public. Salvation's available for everyone! We're being shown how to turn our backs on a godless, indulgent life, and how to take on a God-filled, God-honoring life. This new life is starting right now, and is whetting our appetites for the glorious day when our great God and Savior, Jesus Christ, appears. He offered himself as a sacrifice to free us from a dark, rebellious life into this good, pure life, making us a people he can be proud of, energetic in goodness.

READ

Read the passage aloud slowly.

THINK

Read the passage aloud again, this time picturing the words being spoken by someone you look up to and admire. Which of these rich words or phrases stand out to you? Why do you need these words and ideas at this moment in your life?

Read it one more time, picturing yourself saying the words to someone you wish to encourage.

PRAY

Ask God to guide you in one or all of these movements of growth:

- ☐ turning your back on a "godless, indulgent life"
- ☐ taking on a "God-filled, God-honoring life"
- ☐ believing that "this new life is starting right now"
- ☐ being "energetic in goodness"
- ☐ other:

LIVE

Consider God, who is "energetic in goodness." Inhale that goodness. See how much God wishes to bring you along. Try on the belief that this new life starts right now.

WASHED INSIDE AND OUT

TITUS 3:1-11

1-2 Remind the people to respect the government and be law-abiding, always ready to lend a helping hand. No insults, no fights. God's people should be bighearted and courteous.

3-8 It wasn't so long ago that we ourselves were stupid and stubborn, dupes of sin, ordered every which way by our glands, going around with a chip on our shoulder, hated and hating back. But when God, our kind and loving Savior God, stepped in, he saved us from all that. It was all his doing; we had nothing to do with it. He gave us a good bath, and we came out of it new people, washed inside and out by the Holy Spirit. Our Savior Jesus poured out new life so generously. God's gift has restored our relationship with him and given us back our lives. And there's more life to come — an eternity of life! You can count on this.

8-11 I want you to put your foot down. Take a firm stand on these matters so that those who have put their trust in God will concentrate on the essentials that are good for everyone. Stay away from mindless, pointless quarreling over genealogies and fine print in the law code. That gets you nowhere. Warn a quarrelsome person once or twice, but then be done with him. It's obvious that such a person is out of line, rebellious against God. By persisting in divisiveness he cuts himself off.

READ

Read the passage.

PRAY

What parts of this passage do you react to more than others? Maybe an argument you've had comes to mind, or maybe you have trouble adopting the attitude toward authority described here. Perhaps you wish you could be given a "good bath" and made new. Try to summarize your primary thought. Express it to God.

THINK

Although being purified ("washed inside and out by the Holy Spirit") is good for us and brings wonderfully satisfying results, the process often involves humbling, which isn't easy. Richard Foster said, "Humility means to live as close to the truth as possible: the truth about ourselves, the truth about others, the truth about the world in which we live."[13]

Think about Foster's statement, considering yourself, others, and the world around you. What elements of God's truth in this passage did you have trouble receiving? Maybe you're too hard on yourself and won't believe God's acceptance of you. Maybe you're afraid that if you admit the limitations of someone you look up to, it will unravel everything good you believe about that person. Or maybe you realize you don't want to get close to the real needs and problems of the world. Be open with God about the grime that keeps you from being clean and living closer to the truth.

LIVE

Now, keeping in mind how near or far you live from the truth about yourself, others, and the world, picture God as he's described in this passage: stepping in and washing you inside and out, removing the grime that separates you from the truth. What do you think or feel about that? Whatever surfaces, share it openly with him.

A TRUE CHRISTIAN BROTHER

PHILEMON 8-20

8-9 In line with all this I have a favor to ask of you. As Christ's ambassador and now a prisoner for him, I wouldn't hesitate to command this if I thought it necessary, but I'd rather make it a personal request.

10-14 While here in jail, I've fathered a child, so to speak. And here he is, hand-carrying this letter — Onesimus! He was useless to you before; now he's useful to both of us. I'm sending him back to you, but it feels like I'm cutting off my right arm in doing so. I wanted in the worst way to keep him here as your stand-in to help out while I'm in jail for the Message. But I didn't want to do anything behind your back, make you do a good deed that you hadn't willingly agreed to.

15-16 Maybe it's all for the best that you lost him for a while. You're getting him back now for good — and no mere slave this time, but a true Christian brother! That's what he was to me — he'll be even more than that to you.

17-20 So if you still consider me a comrade-in-arms, welcome him back as you would me. If he damaged anything or owes you anything, chalk it up to my account. This is my personal signature — Paul — and I stand behind it. (I don't need to remind you, do I, that you owe your very life to me?) Do me this big favor, friend. You'll be doing it for Christ, but it will also do my heart good.

READ

Read the passage and, if possible, the entire book of Philemon. (Don't worry — it's only twenty-five verses long!)

THINK

Here Paul writes a letter to Philemon concerning a slave named Onesimus. Paul has grown to see this man as a friend and — more specifically and importantly — as a brother in Christ. So Paul encourages Philemon to accept Onesimus in the same way.

Paul is saying that the greatest label we can have for one another is "true Christian brother" or true Christian sister.

What Christians do you have a hard time accepting as brothers or sisters in Christ? Why is it hard to think of other believers this way? Explore your heart: Is it their backgrounds, ethnicities, behaviors, cultural differences, theological differences, or something else? What would need to change in you for you to accept these people, seeing them as Christian brothers and sisters?

PRAY

Talk to God about this. Tell him about your struggle to accept others. Thank him that he accepts you, and thank him that he sees you and other believers as no less than his very own children. Ask God to help you see others with the same eyes.

LIVE

As you encounter people who are different from you, be reminded that God sees them with the label "my children" — and that means you too.

HOLDING EVERYTHING TOGETHER

HEBREWS 1:3

3 This Son perfectly mirrors God, and is stamped with God's nature. He holds everything together by what he says — powerful words!

READ

Read this verse over and over again. Let it resonate in your heart. Become familiar with the words. Memorize it before moving to the next section.

THINK

Though the authorship of Hebrews is uncertain, we can be certain of the message of the book: God's plan to redeem history came in the form of his Son, Jesus.

Spend time meditating on the passage. First, consider the purpose of a mirror: to display in perfect clarity a faithful representation of an object or person. How incredible to realize that Jesus' role was to be a mirror of God to the world! Second, consider the monumental act of holding *everything* together. How amazing to know that Jesus does this, that he is vital to the vast scope of human history!

In what ways does the significance of Jesus in the world impact your view of him?

PRAY

Stand in front of a mirror and consider Jesus, who mirrors God. While looking at your reflection, ask God for the courage and guidance to help you mirror Jesus to the world, reflecting him as you go about every day.

LIVE

Consider how you might reflect Jesus today — and do it.

DAY 126
_____

GOD ENCOUNTERS

On this seventh day, review and reflect on all you have read this week. Take the time to revel in the ways you've encountered God in the past six days.

RICHES OF GLORY

HEBREWS 2:6-10

6-9 It says in Scripture,

> What is man and woman that you bother with them;
>   why take a second look their way?
> You made them not quite as high as angels,
>   bright with Eden's dawn light;
> Then you put them in charge
>   of your entire handcrafted world.

When God put them in charge of everything, nothing was excluded. But we don't see it yet, don't see everything under human jurisdiction. What we do see is Jesus, made "not quite as high as angels," and then, through the experience of death, crowned so much higher than any angel, with a glory "bright with Eden's dawn light." In that death, by God's grace, he fully experienced death in every person's place.

10 It makes good sense that the God who got everything started and keeps everything going now completes the work by making the Salvation Pioneer perfect through suffering as he leads all these people to glory.

READ

Read the passage aloud slowly.

THINK

Read the passage again, noting the diverse themes of death and suffering versus angels and glory. What words or phrases fascinate you most? Pause a moment and ask God to help you understand them and continue to be absorbed by them. Why do you think those words or phrases fascinate you? What is going on in your life right now — feelings, circumstances, decisions — that they might correspond to?

PRAY

Ask that you will be continually fascinated by God's glory, God's well-deserved honor and brightness.

LIVE

Sit in the quiet and reflect on how you would feel if God were degrading, dishonoring, and not at all beautiful. Why is it better to live and breathe on an earth created by such a magnificent God?

SHARP AS A SURGEON'S SCALPEL

HEBREWS 4:12-13

12-13   God means what he says. What he says goes. His powerful Word is sharp as a surgeon's scalpel, cutting through everything, whether doubt or defense, laying us open to listen and obey. Nothing and no one is impervious to God's Word. We can't get away from it — no matter what.

READ

Read these two verses. Then read verse 13 first (beginning with "Nothing") and verse 12 next. Finally, read the verses in their proper order again.

THINK

Most of us believe that God's Message, his Word, is important. In fact, you probably wouldn't be reading these words right now if you didn't believe God's Word is significant. But if you're like many people, reading it sometimes feels like a chore — less than enjoyable.

Most Jewish children in the first century would memorize the first five books of the Bible (the Pentateuch) before their thirteenth birthdays.[14] They were taught to believe that the words were a love letter to them from God himself.

Think now about how important Scripture is to *you*. What if you were unable to read or hear anything from the Bible for twelve months? Would you miss it? Why or why not? What do you think "no one is impervious to God's Word" means? In what ways have you experienced God's Word to be precise and powerful, "sharp as a surgeon's scalpel"?

PRAY

Start praying by thanking God for the gift of his Word. Ask him to give you more passion and desire for it. Give God permission to let his Word "[lay you] open to listen and obey" in the days and weeks ahead.

LIVE

Memorize these verses, and pray them regularly as a way of asking God to make Scripture increasingly important in your life.

SPIRITUAL LIFELINE

HEBREWS 6:13-19

13-18 When God made his promise to Abraham, he backed it to the hilt, putting his own reputation on the line. He said, "I promise that I'll bless you with everything I have — bless and bless and bless!" Abraham stuck it out and got everything that had been promised to him. When people make promises, they guarantee them by appeal to some authority above them so that if there is any question that they'll make good on the promise, the authority will back them up. When God wanted to guarantee his promises, he gave his word, a rock-solid guarantee — God *can't* break his word. And because his word cannot change, the promise is likewise unchangeable.

18-19 We who have run for our very lives to God have every reason to grab the promised hope with both hands and never let go. It's an unbreakable spiritual lifeline, reaching past all appearances right to the very presence of God.

READ

Read the passage aloud slowly.

THINK

Read the passage aloud again, noting the emphasis on promises and hope. Consider what part hope has played in your life. Its opposites are despair, suspicion, doubt, and cynicism. What does this passage tell you about hope?

Read the passage aloud one more time. What words or phrases stand out to you? Why are those words or phrases important for you today?

PRAY

Pick out phrases that you'd like to pray and converse with God about, such as:

- ☐ "make good on the promise"
- ☐ "his word cannot change"
- ☐ "grab the promised hope"
- ☐ "never let go"

LIVE

Walk through this day trying on an attitude of greater hope — expectancy, anticipation, trust. This is what everyday life in the kingdom of God looks like.

THROWING OUT THE OLD PLAN

HEBREWS 8:1-2,6-12

1-2 In essence, we have just such a high priest: authoritative right alongside God, conducting worship in the one true sanctuary built by God. . . .

6-12 But Jesus' priestly work far surpasses what these other priests do, since he's working from a far better plan. If the first plan — the old covenant — had worked out, a second wouldn't have been needed. But we know the first was found wanting, because God said,

> Heads up! The days are coming
>   when I'll set up a new plan
>   for dealing with Israel and Judah.
> I'll throw out the old plan
>   I set up with their ancestors
>   when I led them by the hand out of Egypt.
> They didn't keep their part of the bargain,
>   so I looked away and let it go.
> This new plan I'm making with Israel
>   isn't going to be written on paper,
>   isn't going to be chiseled in stone;
> This time I'm writing out the plan *in* them,
>   carving it on the lining of their hearts.
> I'll be their God,
>   they'll be my people.
> They won't go to school to learn about me,
>   or buy a book called *God in Five Easy Lessons*.
> They'll all get to know me firsthand,
>   the little and the big, the small and the great.
> They'll get to know me by being kindly forgiven,
>   with the slate of their sins forever wiped clean.

READ

Read the passage from the perspective of someone living in Old Testament times, hearing the promise of a "new plan" that has no form yet. What would life be like without Jesus? Sit and take in this picture of life. Let yourself imagine what it would be like to sin in that context and to relate to God.

THINK

Read the passage again, this time from your present-day perspective, noting contrasts with the Old Testament perspective. What does it mean to you to hear God say he'll "throw out the old plan" that expects you to perfectly obey Old Testament laws? How does this reality make you see Jesus differently? What's it like to have such an approachable high priest to make sure your sins are "wiped clean," to "kindly" forgive you, and to show you what God is like?

PRAY/LIVE

Talk with Jesus about what stands out to you from this time of meditation. Perhaps a new desire to be obedient arises in contrast to previous discouragement over trying to change. Maybe you want to thank Jesus for being near you, or maybe you feel like singing a song of praise to him. Maybe you just want to sit in quiet gratitude because God threw out the "old plan" and wrote out the new plan, "carving it on the lining of [your] heart."

WHAT WE CAN'T SEE

HEBREWS 11:1-3,39-40

1-2   The fundamental fact of existence is that this trust in God, this faith, is the firm foundation under everything that makes life worth living. It's our handle on what we can't see. The act of faith is what distinguished our ancestors, set them above the crowd.

3   By faith, we see the world called into existence by God's word, what we see created by what we don't see. . . .

39-40   Not one of these people, even though their lives of faith were exemplary, got their hands on what was promised. God had a better plan for us: that their faith and our faith would come together to make one completed whole, their lives of faith not complete apart from ours.

READ

If possible, read all of Hebrews 11, but focus on verses 1-3 and 39-40.

THINK

This familiar passage of Scripture is often called the Faith Hall of Fame. It lists people of the Bible who exhibited the faith — sometimes at extreme personal cost — that made God famous. Talking about faith is much easier than living it out every day, but we can turn to these people's lives for inspiration.

You've heard, and possibly even uttered, the saying "Seeing is believing." The writer of Hebrews begins with a definition of faith that he connects to eyesight. Faith, he writes, is "our handle on what we can't see. . . . By faith, we see the world called into existence by God's word, what we see created by what we don't see." So, really, *not* seeing is believing.

What do you have a hard time believing because you can't prove it by seeing or touching it yourself? Would faith be easier if you could physically see the object of your faith? (Would faith still be faith if you could see the object, or would faith cease to be faith and become fact?)

PRAY

Thank God for godly people who inspire you to the kind of faith described in this chapter of the Bible.

LIVE

Sometime today, choose one of the people mentioned in the Faith Hall of Fame and read his or her story in Scripture. (Use a concordance to find the story, if you need to.)

WELL-TRAINED

HEBREWS 12:7-11

7-11 God is educating you; that's why you must never drop out. He's treating you as dear children. This trouble you're in isn't punishment; it's *training*, the normal experience of children. Only irresponsible parents leave children to fend for themselves. Would you prefer an irresponsible God? We respect our own parents for training and not spoiling us, so why not embrace God's training so we can truly *live*? While we were children, our parents did what *seemed* best to them. But God is doing what *is* best for us, training us to live God's holy best. At the time, discipline isn't much fun. It always feels like it's going against the grain. Later, of course, it pays off handsomely, for it's the well-trained who find themselves mature in their relationship with God.

READ

Read the passage aloud slowly.

THINK

Read the passage again.

How might God use the "trouble you're in" to *train* you? Don't jump on the first thing that comes to mind. Sit quietly for a while and see what God brings to you.

How might you cooperate better in this training? Once again, the first thing that comes to mind might not be God, but an old tape from the past. So take time to listen.

PRAY

Tell God what sort of well-trained person you'd like to be. What would you look like? Express confidence that this picture would be a much better life for you.

LIVE

Try to crawl into the persona of the well-trained person you'd like to become. How would your burdens in life be lighter?

DAY 133

GOD ENCOUNTERS

On this seventh day, review and reflect on all you have read this week. Take the time to revel in the ways you've encountered God in the past six days.

BE RELAXED WITH WHAT YOU HAVE

HEBREWS 13:5-9

5-6   Don't be obsessed with getting more material things. Be relaxed with what you have. Since God assured us, "I'll never let you down, never walk off and leave you," we can boldly quote,

> God is there, ready to help;
> I'm fearless no matter what.
> Who or what can get to me?

7-8   Appreciate your pastoral leaders who gave you the Word of God. Take a good look at the way they live, and let their faithfulness instruct you, as well as their truthfulness. There should be a consistency that runs through us all. For Jesus doesn't change — yesterday, today, tomorrow, he's always totally himself.

9   Don't be lured away from him by the latest speculations about him. The grace of Christ is the only good ground for life. Products named after Christ don't seem to do much for those who buy them.

READ
Read the passage aloud.

THINK
Spend time pondering the connection the writer is making between obsession with material possessions and the belief that God might leave us or let us down. What do you make of this? How are the two ideas related to each other?

PRAY
Take several minutes to explore your life in light of this instruction. How do you relate to material things? Do you often wish you had more? Do you feel that nothing can harm you because of what you have? What fears do you have about God letting you down? What would it be like to "be relaxed with what you have"? Talk with him about this subject. Attentively listen for his input.

LIVE
Continue praying by personalizing the verses, pausing frequently to notice your internal reaction to what you're saying. For example, *God, help me avoid being obsessed with getting more material things. I want to be relaxed with what I have, since you assured me . . .*"

When you're finished, look through the passage one more time, honestly confessing the contrary reactions, if any, you experienced when praying. With each, become aware of the possibility that your contrary feeling or belief could change. (Don't try to force that change; just be aware of the possibility.) For example, you could repeat to your soul that "God is there, ready to help," or you could ask God to increase your belief that he'll "never walk off and leave you."

ACT ON WHAT YOU HEAR

JAMES 1:19-27

19-21 Post this at all the intersections, dear friends: Lead with your ears, follow up with your tongue, and let anger straggle along in the rear. God's righteousness doesn't grow from human anger. So throw all spoiled virtue and cancerous evil in the garbage. In simple humility, let our gardener, God, landscape you with the Word, making a salvation-garden of your life.

22-24 Don't fool yourself into thinking that you are a listener when you are anything but, letting the Word go in one ear and out the other. *Act* on what you hear! Those who hear and don't act are like those who glance in the mirror, walk away, and two minutes later have no idea who they are, what they look like.

25 But whoever catches a glimpse of the revealed counsel of God — the free life! — even out of the corner of his eye, and sticks with it, is no distracted scatterbrain but a man or woman of action. That person will find delight and affirmation in the action.

26-27 Anyone who sets himself up as "religious" by talking a good game is self-deceived. This kind of religion is hot air and only hot air. Real religion, the kind that passes muster before God the Father, is this: Reach out to the homeless and loveless in their plight, and guard against corruption from the godless world.

READ

Meditate on this passage. Underline words or phrases that stick out to you. Circle repeated words.

THINK

Consider what roles specific body parts have in your spiritual formation. James says here that our lives as followers of Jesus can be shaped by how we choose to use (or refrain from using) our ears and our tongue.

How have your ears and tongue been beneficial or damaging to your interactions with others recently? Be specific. When have you said one thing and done the other? Think about what James says about that.

PRAY

Start your time of communication with God by putting your hands on your ears and saying aloud, "God, I desire to listen to what you want me to hear."

Remain in the silence. (You can lower your hands.)

Now put your hands over your mouth and say aloud, "God, I desire to use my tongue to speak words that are helpful and to refrain from speaking words that are hurtful."

Remain in the silence.

Confess those times when you have not listened and when you have spoken unnecessary and harmful words.

Remain in the silence.

LIVE

In conversations today, be mindful of the percentage of time you are speaking compared to the time you are listening to others. Then ask yourself whether the percentage is healthy.

SO-CALLED IMPORTANT PEOPLE

JAMES 2:1-9

1-4   My dear friends, don't let public opinion influence how you live out our glorious, Christ-originated faith. If a man enters your church wearing an expensive suit, and a street person wearing rags comes in right after him, and you say to the man in the suit, "Sit here, sir; this is the best seat in the house!" and either ignore the street person or say, "Better sit here in the back row," haven't you segregated God's children and proved that you are judges who can't be trusted?

5-7   Listen, dear friends. Isn't it clear by now that God operates quite differently? He chose the world's down-and-out as the kingdom's first citizens, with full rights and privileges. This kingdom is promised to anyone who loves God. And here you are abusing these same citizens! Isn't it the high and mighty who exploit you, who use the courts to rob you blind? Aren't they the ones who scorn the new name — "Christian" — used in your baptisms?

8-9   You do well when you complete the Royal Rule of the Scriptures: "Love others as you love yourself." But if you play up to these so-called important people, you go against the Rule and stand convicted by it.

READ

Read the passage aloud slowly. Who are the "so-called important people" in your life? (They don't have to be wealthy, but just people you want to impress or want to think highly of you.)

THINK

Read the passage again, noticing these words: *ignore, segregate, exploit, scorn.* James is urging us to love people and use things (as opposed to loving things and using people).

1. Whom do you "use" to entertain you? To help you? To make you feel better?
2. What does it look like to love others as you love yourself? To give others the same amount of time, energy, and attention you give yourself?

Set aside these thoughts and read the passage one more time. What comes to you from this passage? What might God be saying to you today?

PRAY

Pray for those in your life you are tempted to use. Ask God to show you how to care for them the way you already care for yourself.

LIVE

Sit quietly, picturing Jesus greeting people he encountered with great love (he never used anyone). What feeling did each person have in his presence? Feel that. You are in his presence now.

WISE LIVING

JAMES 3:13-18

13-16   Do you want to be counted wise, to build a reputation for wisdom? Here's what you do: Live well, live wisely, live humbly. It's the way you live, not the way you talk, that counts. Mean-spirited ambition isn't wisdom. Boasting that you are wise isn't wisdom. Twisting the truth to make yourselves sound wise isn't wisdom. It's the furthest thing from wisdom — it's animal cunning, devilish conniving. Whenever you're trying to look better than others or get the better of others, things fall apart and everyone ends up at the others' throats.

17-18   Real wisdom, God's wisdom, begins with a holy life and is characterized by getting along with others. It is gentle and reasonable, overflowing with mercy and blessings, not hot one day and cold the next, not two-faced. You can develop a healthy, robust community that lives right with God and enjoy its results *only* if you do the hard work of getting along with each other, treating each other with dignity and honor.

READ

Stand up and read the passage. Then read it a second time.

THINK

Defining something accurately involves stating what it is and what it is not. James does just that, telling us what wisdom is and is not. Review the passage again. Make two columns on a piece of paper, and in your own words write in one column what James says wisdom is not. Then in the other column write what James says wisdom is.

How do these characteristics of wisdom (and the lack thereof) line up with your actions recently? If James followed you around and observed your life for a week, what comments might he make about the presence — or absence — of wisdom? James says that wisdom is hard work. In what ways do you see it as hard work?

PRAY

Tell God your desire to become wise, to "do the hard work of getting along with each other." Ask him to help you.

LIVE

Ask a friend or family member you trust to give you honest feedback for the next few weeks about wisdom in your life. Give them permission to affirm wise areas of your life and wise decisions you make, as well as to point out unwise areas of your life and unwise decisions you make.

A LOUD NO . . .
A QUIET YES

JAMES 4:7-10

7-10 So let God work his will in you. Yell a loud *no* to the Devil and watch him scamper. Say a quiet *yes* to God and he'll be there in no time. Quit dabbling in sin. Purify your inner life. Quit playing the field. Hit bottom, and cry your eyes out. The fun and games are over. Get serious, really serious. Get down on your knees before the Master; it's the only way you'll get on your feet.

READ

This is a short passage of contrasts. Read the entire thing aloud. Read it again, this time reading every other sentence aloud. Read it again, this time reading the other sentences aloud. Then read it again in its entirety.

THINK

Someone has said that we usually think of Satan in one of two ways: We either give him too much credit for his work in the world or we don't give him any credit at all. Neither view is right. James tells us that we are to "yell a loud *no* to the Devil and watch him scamper." So this means the Devil is active, but it also means that yelling no at him by Jesus' power in us is enough to scare him away.

In what ways have you seen Satan work destructively in your life, in the lives of others around you, and in the world? What do you think your practical response should be to the Devil's work?

James also tells us to "say a quiet *yes* to God and he'll be there in no time." Think about the times you need to say that "quiet *yes*" for God to come to you.

PRAY

Are you tempted to sin? Shout a loud *no* to Satan and be assured that he will leave you alone.

Are you in need of God's comfort and promises in your life? Whisper that you need him and be assured that he is at your side.

Rest in God's promises in Scripture.

LIVE

Remember the power that God has in your life and over the Devil. Live confidently that in Christ we always win, which means we don't have to be afraid. Utilize the tools of "a loud *no*" and "a quiet *yes*" in your walk with Jesus.

HEALED INSIDE AND OUT

JAMES 5:13-18

13-15   Are you hurting? Pray. Do you feel great? Sing. Are you sick? Call the church leaders together to pray and anoint you with oil in the name of the Master. Believing-prayer will heal you, and Jesus will put you on your feet. And if you've sinned, you'll be forgiven — healed inside and out.

16-18   Make this your common practice: Confess your sins to each other and pray for each other so that you can live together whole and healed. The prayer of a person living right with God is something powerful to be reckoned with. Elijah, for instance, human just like us, prayed hard that it wouldn't rain, and it didn't — not a drop for three and a half years. Then he prayed that it would rain, and it did. The showers came and everything started growing again.

READ

Read the passage aloud slowly.

THINK

Read the passage aloud again. What is God inviting you to do or be in this passage? How does this invitation resonate with what's going on in your life right now? Where are you hurting or sick or in need of forgiveness? Where do you need to sing?

PRAY

Offer a "believing-prayer"—one that trusts God. Confess your sins to God, and ask him if there is someone you could confess to so "you can live together whole and healed." If there is, ask God for the courage to speak to the person about it.

LIVE

Try to live in the reality that you are freshly confessed—whole and healed inside and out. What does that look like in your life today?

DAY 140

GOD ENCOUNTERS

On this seventh day, review and reflect on all you have read this week. Take the time to revel in the ways you've encountered God in the past six days.

A DEEP CONSCIOUSNESS OF GOD

1 PETER 1:13-22

13-16   So roll up your sleeves, put your mind in gear, be totally ready to receive the gift that's coming when Jesus arrives. Don't lazily slip back into those old grooves of evil, doing just what you feel like doing. You didn't know any better then; you do now. As obedient children, let yourselves be pulled into a way of life shaped by God's life, a life energetic and blazing with holiness. God said, "I am holy; you be holy."

17   You call out to God for help and he helps — he's a good Father that way. But don't forget, he's also a responsible Father, and won't let you get by with sloppy living.

18-21   Your life is a journey you must travel with a deep consciousness of God. It cost God plenty to get you out of that dead-end, empty-headed life you grew up in. He paid with Christ's sacred blood, you know. He died like an unblemished, sacrificial lamb. And this was no afterthought. Even though it has only lately — at the end of the ages — become public knowledge, God always knew he was going to do this for you. It's because of this sacrificed Messiah, whom God then raised from the dead and glorified, that you trust God, that you know you have a future in God.

22   Now that you've cleaned up your lives by following the truth, love one another as if your lives depended on it.

READ

Read this passage, and the expanded passage, if possible.

THINK

Peter, the young apostle who denied Jesus during the last hours of Jesus' life, is now a grown man and mature Christ-follower. Here he writes words of encouragement and wisdom to other followers of Jesus.

Peter talks about being holy, meaning different, separate, set apart. He encourages followers to live differently from how the world lives — with "a deep consciousness of God." What would it mean for your life's journey to travel through it with that "deep consciousness"?

What does "let yourselves be pulled into a way of life shaped by God's life" mean, practically? It sounds good, but what would it mean to really live that way?

Peter instructs, "Love one another as if your lives depended on it." What would loving others this way require of you?

PRAY

Let these phrases guide your prayer life right now:

- "I am holy; you be holy."
- "You must travel with a deep consciousness of God."
- "Let [yourself] be pulled into a way of life shaped by God's life."
- "Love one another as if your [life] depended on it."

LIVE

Ask God for a way to live separately, differently, and uniquely from the way the world lives.

THE KIND OF LIFE CHRIST LIVED

1 PETER 2:11-17,21

11-12   Friends, this world is not your home, so don't make yourselves cozy in it. Don't indulge your ego at the expense of your soul. Live an exemplary life among the natives so that your actions will refute their prejudices. Then they'll be won over to God's side and be there to join in the celebration when he arrives.

13-17   Make the Master proud of you by being good citizens. Respect the authorities, whatever their level; they are God's emissaries for keeping order. It is God's will that by doing good, you might cure the ignorance of the fools who think you're a danger to society. Exercise your freedom by serving God, not by breaking the rules. Treat everyone you meet with dignity. Love your spiritual family. Revere God. Respect the government. . . .

21   This is the kind of life you've been invited into, the kind of life Christ lived. He suffered everything that came his way so you would know that it could be done, and also know how to do it, step-by-step.

READ

Read the passage aloud slowly.

THINK

Read the passage again aloud, noting what "the kind of life you've been invited into, the kind of life Christ lived" looks like.

1. What, if anything, in this description of "the kind of life Christ lived" surprises you?
2. What, if anything, in this description fits with what you've been doing lately?
3. What, if anything, in this description challenges you?
4. Consider the day you have in front of you. How might the ideas of respect, celebration, and living Christ's life fit into it?

PRAY

Thank God for the rich "kind of life Christ lived." Ask God to draw you more deeply into that ongoing, vibrant life of Christ. Add anything else that came to you during today's meditation.

LIVE

Rest and delight in living "the kind of life Christ lived" today. Consider that you won't be bored; rather, it will be an adventure.

IN ADORATION

1 PETER 3:13-18

13-18 If with heart and soul you're doing good, do you think you can be stopped? Even if you suffer for it, you're still better off. Don't give the opposition a second thought. Through thick and thin, keep your hearts at attention, in adoration before Christ, your Master. Be ready to speak up and tell anyone who asks why you're living the way you are, and always with the utmost courtesy. Keep a clear conscience before God so that when people throw mud at you, none of it will stick. They'll end up realizing that *they're* the ones who need a bath. It's better to suffer for doing good, if that's what God wants, than to be punished for doing bad. That's what Christ did definitively: suffered because of others' sins, the Righteous One for the unrighteous ones. He went through it all — was put to death and then made alive — to bring us to God.

READ

Read this passage a few times, slowly and meditatively.

THINK

Mull over Peter's exhortation to adore Christ in every kind of circumstance. Do you agree with the link he makes between adoring Christ and doing good to others? When you're relating to others, what kinds of things do you give your attention to, if not to adoring Christ? Do you have other goals, like giving the person a good impression of you or making useful connections? In what ways does this approach to relationships leave you satisfied or dissatisfied?

PRAY

Share with Jesus what has surfaced for you, remembering that he, "the Righteous One," already knows the unrighteousness in you, and "went through it all" for you anyway: He loves you.

Sit with him in silence. Even if you don't sense him saying anything, that's okay. Just stay there, open to him. If you are led to genuine adoration of him, go ahead and take time to tell him what you think of him. If not, just receive his acceptance of you.

LIVE

Douglas Steere, a leading Quaker of the twentieth century, once said, "In the school of adoration the soul learns why the approach to every other goal has left it restless."[15] Think back to how you relate to others and notice any dissatisfaction or restlessness in that. What would it look like for you to give Peter's idea a shot: to walk through today "in adoration before Christ"? Try it.

NO LONGER TYRANNIZED

1 PETER 4:1-2,14,19

1-2 Since Jesus went through everything you're going through and more, learn to think like him. Think of your sufferings as a weaning from that old sinful habit of always expecting to get your own way. Then you'll be able to live out your days free to pursue what God wants instead of being tyrannized by what you want. . . .

14 If you're abused because of Christ, count yourself fortunate. It's the Spirit of God and his glory in you that brought you to the notice of others. . . .

19 So if you find life difficult because you're doing what God said, take it in stride. Trust him. He knows what he's doing, and he'll keep on doing it.

READ
Read the passage aloud slowly.

THINK
Read verses 1-2 again slowly. How does any suffering (which may be more like disappointment or frustration) you're going through relate to "being tyrannized by what you want," for example, wanting your own way but not getting it? In what ways does your "wanter" (the part of you that decides what you want) need to be invited to change?

Read verses 14 and 19 again slowly. Are you being discounted or badly treated because you're living a selfless, Christlike life? If so, in what ways? If not, how might that happen to you at some point?

PRAY
Ask the Holy Spirit to fill you and help you change the deep desires inside you. If you're being mistreated because of Christ, ask the Holy Spirit to help you absorb the truth that the Spirit and his glory is what brought you to the notice of others.

LIVE
Picture yourself as one who has "the Spirit of God and his glory in you" so you will come "to the notice of others." Consider that such a suffering life is intimately linked with God and provides the companionship of the Spirit.

BUILDING ON WHAT YOU'VE BEEN GIVEN

2 PETER 1:3-9

3-4 Everything that goes into a life of pleasing God has been miraculously given to us by getting to know, personally and intimately, the One who invited us to God. The best invitation we ever received! We were also given absolutely terrific promises to pass on to you — your tickets to participation in the life of God after you turned your back on a world corrupted by lust.

5-9 So don't lose a minute in building on what you've been given, complementing your basic faith with good character, spiritual understanding, alert discipline, passionate patience, reverent wonder, warm friendliness, and generous love, each dimension fitting into and developing the others. With these qualities active and growing in your lives, no grass will grow under your feet, no day will pass without its reward as you mature in your experience of our Master Jesus. Without these qualities you can't see what's right before you, oblivious that your old sinful life has been wiped off the books.

READ

Go into a room by yourself and close the door behind you, then read the passage aloud.

THINK

A God-pleasing life has been given to us by an intimate relationship with Christ himself. And Peter reminds us of our "best invitation" to participate in God's amazing, all-encompassing plan to redeem the world! Peter says we should complement our "basic faith" with the following:

- "good character"
- "spiritual understanding"
- "alert discipline"
- "passionate patience"
- "reverent wonder"
- "warm friendliness"
- "generous love"

Take your time to ponder each character trait. Then think about those you are doing well in. Think about those you need to grow in.

PRAY

Admit your need for God's guidance and help in your growth in him. Ask him to help you grow in those areas where you recognize you need the most improvement.

LIVE

On a small sheet of paper, write down the character traits you desire to develop. Review often what you wrote.

Ask the Holy Spirit for encouragement — to illuminate and reveal areas of your life that show these character traits when they become evident.

DESTRUCTIVE DIVISIONS

2 PETER 2:1-3

1-2   But there were also *lying* prophets among the people then, just as there will be lying religious teachers among you. They'll smuggle in destructive divisions, pitting you against each other — biting the hand of the One who gave them a chance to have their lives back! They've put themselves on a fast downhill slide to destruction, but not before they recruit a crowd of mixed-up followers who can't tell right from wrong.

2-3   They give the way of truth a bad name. They're only out for themselves. They'll say anything, *anything*, that sounds good to exploit you. They won't, of course, get by with it. They'll come to a bad end, for God has never just stood by and let that kind of thing go on.

READ

Read the passage aloud slowly.

THINK

Read the passage again slowly, noticing what causes destructive divisions. Keep in mind that the people who cause divisions rarely realize they're doing it. They may have good intentions (or *think* they have them) because they believe they're right about something.

1. Where have you witnessed destructive divisions within the body of Christ lately?
2. How might you grieve over having witnessed people:

   - pitting other people against one another
   - biting the hand that helped them
   - looking out for only themselves (even if unconsciously)
   - exploiting other people for their own cause

3. In what ways do such destructive divisions *lie* (see verse 1) to the world about who God is and what God is like?
4. What might God be leading you to pray? What sort of person might God be leading you to *be*?

PRAY

Thank God for doing what he promises in this passage: never standing by and letting destructive divisions go on. Ask God to show you how you are not to stand by, but to be one who prays for the injured as well as the "*lying* prophets" — for both to grasp truth and love and to find healing.

LIVE

Grieve with God over people's willingness to create divisions within the church, which embodies the noncompetitive unity of the Trinity.

DAY 147

GOD ENCOUNTERS

On this seventh day, review and reflect on all you have read this week. Take the time to revel in the ways you've encountered God in the past six days.

IF ANYONE DOES SIN

1 JOHN 1:6–2:2

6-7 If we claim that we experience a shared life with him and continue to stumble around in the dark, we're obviously lying through our teeth — we're not *living* what we claim. But if we walk in the light, God himself being the light, we also experience a shared life with one another, as the sacrificed blood of Jesus, God's Son, purges all our sin.

8-10 If we claim that we're free of sin, we're only fooling ourselves. A claim like that is errant nonsense. On the other hand, if we admit our sins — make a clean breast of them — he won't let us down; he'll be true to himself. He'll forgive our sins and purge us of all wrongdoing. If we claim that we've never sinned, we out-and-out contradict God — make a liar out of him. A claim like that only shows off our ignorance of God.

1-2 I write this, dear children, to guide you out of sin. But if anyone does sin, we have a Priest-Friend in the presence of the Father: Jesus Christ, righteous Jesus. When he served as a sacrifice for our sins, he solved the sin problem for good — not only ours, but the whole world's.

READ

Read the passage.

THINK

Truth. Grace. The two sides of a fence we often fall off of when responding to sin. In going to one extreme, we might rebuke sin but leave the sinner feeling condemned or rejected. In going to the other extreme, we might communicate acceptance to the sinner but minimize the sin, leaving the sinner in its bondage. John's perspective is different.

Look at the two halves of the problem presented in this passage: our attitude toward sin and our expectations of how God views sin. Notice what John points out about the role the Father and Jesus each play in the situation and the choice we have in how we view ourselves. Take a few moments to let John's statements about these things sink into you.

PRAY

What is your attitude toward the sins with which you struggle? What deeper desire lies beneath the draw that particular sin has on you? Does your guilt hold you back from Jesus? Talk to him about this.

Now sit silently, listening for Jesus' response to you. What is his desire for you?

LIVE

Consider a situation that holds temptation for you. Ask Jesus to remind you of his presence as Priest-Friend the next time you're faced with that temptation.

LET'S NOT JUST TALK ABOUT LOVE

1 JOHN 3:16-24

16-17   This is how we've come to understand and experience love: Christ sacrificed his life for us. This is why we ought to live sacrificially for our fellow believers, and not just be out for ourselves. If you see some brother or sister in need and have the means to do something about it but turn a cold shoulder and do nothing, what happens to God's love? It disappears. And you made it disappear.

18-20   My dear children, let's not just talk about love; let's practice real love. This is the only way we'll know we're living truly, living in God's reality. It's also the way to shut down debilitating self-criticism, even when there is something to it. For God is greater than our worried hearts and knows more about us than we do ourselves.

21-24   And friends, once that's taken care of and we're no longer accusing or condemning ourselves, we're bold and free before God! We're able to stretch our hands out and receive what we asked for because we're doing what he said, doing what pleases him. Again, this is God's command: to believe in his personally named Son, Jesus Christ. He told us to love each other, in line with the original command. As we keep his commands, we live deeply and surely in him, and he lives in us. And this is how we experience his deep and abiding presence in us: by the Spirit he gave us.

READ

Read the passage slowly and carefully until you understand the crux of John's argument: that we can cease to be controlled by the internal voice of self-criticism when we love others.

PRAY

What role does self-criticism play in your life? Maybe there's that voice in your head constantly telling you what you *should* have done. Maybe you can instantly think of six aspects of yourself that you'd change if you could. Maybe receiving compliments or affirmation from others is hard for you. Explore this with God, and talk with him about what you find. Be open to what he might want to show you about yourself.

THINK

Why do you think John so firmly ties together loving other people and freedom from self-criticism? Ponder this connection. In what ways are the two related?

Become aware of how much you do and do not believe John's argument. Be honest with yourself and with God, remembering that it's okay to admit that, while you think something sounds true, you aren't sure you believe it.

LIVE

Pay special attention today to how much you criticize yourself or minimize praise given by others. Notice what runs through your head when you look in the mirror or if you beat yourself up over mistakes at work. Jot these things down if you need help remembering. Then, sometime later in the day, talk to God for a few minutes about what you are noticing. Recall what John says about loving others and self-criticism, and ponder it some more.

GOD'S INDWELLING LOVE

1 JOHN 4:7,11-13,16-18

7   My beloved friends, let us continue to love each other since love comes from God. Everyone who loves is born of God and experiences a relationship with God. . . .

11-12   My dear, dear friends, if God loved us like this, we certainly ought to love each other. No one has seen God, ever. But if we love one another, God dwells deeply within us, and his love becomes complete in us — perfect love!

13,16   This is how we know we're living steadily and deeply in him, and he in us: He's given us life from his life, from his very own Spirit. . . . We know it so well, we've embraced it heart and soul, this love that comes from God.

17-18   God is love. When we take up permanent residence in a life of love, we live in God and God lives in us. This way, love has the run of the house, becomes at home and mature in us, so that we're free of worry on Judgment Day — our standing in the world is identical with Christ's. There is no room in love for fear. Well-formed love banishes fear. Since fear is crippling, a fearful life — fear of death, fear of judgment — is one not yet fully formed in love.

READ

Read the passage aloud slowly.

THINK

Read the passage again slowly, pausing after the word *love* each time you read it aloud. While the command to love one another can be difficult, consider also these things that empower people to love one another:

- "Love comes from God."
- We experience a relationship with God.
- We receive love from God, so we're turning that love around to others.
- "God dwells deeply within us."
- God gives us his life.
- God gives us the Spirit.
- God lives in us and we live in God.
- The love we've already experienced is chasing away fear, which often keeps us from loving others.

1. Which of the above ideas is the easiest for you to grasp? Why?
2. Which one is the most difficult for you to grasp? Why?

Draw a little stick figure of yourself as the recipient of what is being given (love or relationship or God's own life or the Spirit).

3. How does it feel to receive like this?

PRAY

Thank God for pouring into you such things (your answers to 1 and 2, the entire list, or other phrases in the passage). Express your desire to be saturated with God's love so it overflows in you and pours out to others. (Or express the desire to have that desire.)

LIVE

Contemplate yourself as an absorber and container of God's love, as one who is taking up permanent residence in a life of love.

PROOF THAT WE LOVE GOD

1 JOHN 5:1-3

1-3   Every person who believes that Jesus is, in fact, the Messiah, is God-begotten. If we love the One who conceives the child, we'll surely love the child who was conceived. The reality test on whether or not we love God's children is this: Do we love God? Do we keep his commands? The proof that we love God comes when we keep his commandments and they are not at all troublesome.

READ

Read the passage three times slowly.

THINK

What do you think of this connection between loving God and loving others? Does one or the other feel more difficult for you? Which one? What about it is difficult?

PRAY

Talk to God about the difficulties you experience in this area. Openly share with him your feelings about your struggle. Listen for what he might have to say.

LIVE

C. S. Lewis wrote, "It may be possible for each of us to think too much of his own potential glory hereafter; it is hardly possible for him to think too often or too deeply about that of his neighbor.... The dullest and most uninteresting person you talk to may one day be a creature which, if you saw it now, you would be strongly tempted to worship.... There are no ordinary people."[16] How does this suggestion alter the way you view others you know? How does it alter the way you view yourself? As you go through your day, ponder these ideas more, but also be ready to ponder-in-practice: As you come across "God's children" during the day, look for small ways to love them.

LIVING OUT THE TRUTH

2 JOHN 4-6

4-6   I can't tell you how happy I am to learn that many members of your congregation are diligent in living out the Truth, exactly as commanded by the Father. But permit me a reminder, friends, and this is not a new commandment but simply a repetition of our original and basic charter: that we love each other. Love means following his commandments, and his unifying commandment is that you conduct your lives in love. This is the first thing you heard, and nothing has changed.

READ

Focus on these verses, but read all of 2 John, if possible.

THINK

If you grew up in the church, you know that love is a critical ingredient in the life of a follower of Jesus. This ingredient may seem elementary, and believers often talk about love. But that's for good reason: Love is the very nature of God! John reminds us: "Love means following his commandments, and his unifying commandment is that you conduct your lives in love. This is the first thing you heard, and nothing has changed."

On a scale of one to ten (with one being the lowest and ten being the highest), how would you rank your "love quotient"? How might your friends rank your love quotient? What is needed for you to grow in your understanding and expression of love to others?

What would your life look like if you were "diligent in living out the Truth"?

PRAY

Ask God to help you see the direct correlation between love and following his commands.

LIVE

Love God. Study his commands. Follow them.

HOSPITALITY WORTHY OF GOD HIMSELF

3 JOHN 5-11

5-8   Dear friend, when you extend hospitality to Christian brothers and sisters, even when they are strangers, you make the faith visible. They've made a full report back to the church here, a message about your love. It's good work you're doing, helping these travelers on their way, hospitality worthy of God himself! They set out under the banner of the Name, and get no help from unbelievers. So they deserve any support we can give them. In providing meals and a bed, we become their companions in spreading the Truth.

9-10   Earlier I wrote something along this line to the church, but Diotrephes, who loves being in charge, denigrates my counsel. If I come, you can be sure I'll hold him to account for spreading vicious rumors about us.

As if that weren't bad enough, he not only refuses hospitality to traveling Christians but tries to stop others from welcoming them. Worse yet, instead of inviting them in he throws them out.

11   Friend, don't go along with evil. Model the good. The person who does good does God's work. The person who does evil falsifies God, doesn't know the first thing about God.

READ

Read the passage carefully, imagining that John is writing specifically to you.

THINK

What opportunity have you had recently to show someone hospitality or in some way help someone who is trying to do good? How did you respond to that opportunity? What do you notice about the motives and priorities behind your action (or nonaction)?

PRAY

Lay before God what you have remembered about that opportunity and what you have discovered in your heart. Maybe you will rejoice with him about the victory you experienced in overcoming a temptation to be greedy or mean-spirited, or perhaps you will feel sadness at a missed opportunity.

LIVE

Brainstorm with God what it might look like for you to take steps toward being more hospitable to others. Think about some gifts you have to offer to others (such as your good cooking, your listening ear, your encouragement). Perhaps some of your gifts you are glad to share, while others you're hesitant to offer to others. Regardless of how you feel about each gift, write down what you have that could be helpful to someone.

Now think of a specific person who would be helped by your hospitality. Offer your list to God, and ask him what he would have you offer to this person. Don't force yourself to give something you can give only grudgingly; remember, "God loves it when the giver delights in the giving" (2 Corinthians 9:7). Be open to take this small step toward hospitality, and be open to how God may change your heart as you do it.

DAY 154

GOD ENCOUNTERS

On this seventh day, review and reflect on all you have read this week. Take the time to revel in the ways you've encountered God in the past six days.

GRACE VERSUS LICENSE

JUDE 3-8

3-4   Dear friends, I've dropped everything to write you about this life of salvation that we have in common. I have to write insisting — begging! — that you fight with everything you have in you for this faith entrusted to us as a gift to guard and cherish. What has happened is that some people have infiltrated our ranks (our Scriptures warned us this would happen), who beneath their pious skin are shameless scoundrels. Their design is to replace the sheer grace of our God with sheer license — which means doing away with Jesus Christ, our one and only Master.

5-7   I'm laying this out as clearly as I can, even though you once knew all this well enough and shouldn't need reminding. Here it is in brief: The Master saved a people out of the land of Egypt. Later he destroyed those who defected. And you know the story of the angels who didn't stick to their post, abandoning it for other, darker missions. But they are now chained and jailed in a black hole until the great Judgment Day. Sodom and Gomorrah, which went to sexual rack and ruin along with the surrounding cities that acted just like them, are another example. Burning and burning and never burning up, they serve still as a stock warning.

8   This is exactly the same program of these latest infiltrators: dirty sex, rule and rulers thrown out, glory dragged in the mud.

READ

Read these verses aloud, including all the passion you sense from Jude.

THINK

Think about the meaning of *license,* or *lawlessness.* Now compare that to what you know *grace* to be. What differences do you see between them?

PRAY

Sit in silence and think back on experiences you've had with license — times you've done whatever you felt like, turning your back on what was right. Now consider experiences you've had with grace. Ask God to show you one of these experiences to focus on. Recall the details: What was it like for you? What was going on around you? What were you feeling about what you'd done wrong?

If you focus on an experience of grace, recall how God made that grace known to you — maybe through another person or through something you read. What did it feel like to be presented with that option? What was it like to take God up on his grace?

If you focus on an experience of license (when you did not open up to God's grace), were you aware of any other options at the time? What motivated you to choose the route you took? What did you feel later, after the dust had settled?

LIVE

Ask God what he wants you to take away from this time with him and his Word. Be assured that "every detail in our lives of love for God is worked into something good" (Romans 8:28). This doesn't mean that we'll feel happy right away or all the time but that God does want to see us restored. Walk through today pondering the grace of this reality.

THE SOVEREIGN-STRONG

REVELATION 1:4-8

4-7 I, John, am writing this to the seven churches in Asia province: All the best to you from THE GOD WHO IS, THE GOD WHO WAS, AND THE GOD ABOUT TO ARRIVE, and from the Seven Spirits assembled before his throne, and from Jesus Christ — Loyal Witness, Firstborn from the dead, Ruler of all earthly kings.

> Glory and strength to Christ, who loves us,
>   who blood-washed our sins from our lives,
> Who made us a Kingdom, Priests for his Father,
>   forever — and yes, he's on his way!
> Riding the clouds, he'll be seen by every eye,
>   those who mocked and killed him will see him,
> People from all nations and all times
>   will tear their clothes in lament.
>   Oh, Yes.

8 The Master declares, "I'm A to Z. I'm THE GOD WHO IS, THE GOD WHO WAS, AND THE GOD ABOUT TO ARRIVE. I'm the Sovereign-Strong."

THINK

Revelation is a surreal book, full of visions and events that usually stir up more questions than answers. But from one perspective, the book is not as complex as it seems. Revelation displays the final piece of God's magnificent and victorious story for people. In short, the book could be summarized with two words: God wins. And because of this, it propels us into overwhelming gratitude. Revelation is about worship.

READ

Read the passage aloud, noting the characteristics and actions of God.

PRAY

Lie on your back in stillness (outside, if possible, where you can see the sky). Focus on the magnificence of God's character and how he brings victory to humanity. As you think about who God is, whisper these words to him:

> God, you are A to Z.
> God, you are The God Who Is.
> God, you are The God Who Was.
> God, you are The God About to Arrive.
> God, you are the Sovereign-Strong.

Express your gratitude to God in whatever heartfelt way you wish.

LIVE

Live your life today in complete and total thankfulness for who God is and for the plan he's had in mind all along. Use your life as a palette to display your grateful response to him as the victorious Sovereign-Strong.

LISTEN

REVELATION 2:7,10-11,17

7   "Are your ears awake? Listen. Listen to the Wind Words, the Spirit blowing through the churches. I'm about to call each conqueror to dinner. I'm spreading a banquet of Tree-of-Life fruit, a supper plucked from God's orchard." . . .

10   "Fear nothing in the things you're about to suffer — but stay on guard! Fear nothing! The Devil is about to throw you in jail for a time of testing — ten days. It won't last forever.

   "Don't quit, even if it costs you your life. Stay there believing. I have a Life-Crown sized and ready for you.

11   "Are your ears awake? Listen. Listen to the Wind Words, the Spirit blowing through the churches. Christ-conquerors are safe from Devil-death." . . .

17   "Are your ears awake? Listen. Listen to the Wind Words, the Spirit blowing through the churches. I'll give the sacred manna to every conqueror; I'll also give a clear, smooth stone inscribed with your new name, your secret new name."

READ

Read the passage aloud slowly.

THINK

Sit down (if you aren't already sitting). Read the passage aloud again, standing up each time you read, "Are your ears awake? Listen. Listen to the Wind Words, the Spirit blowing through the churches."

When you're finished, stand up again and ponder what God might have been trying to say to you recently about your life with him, about your behavior toward others, about your deepest self, about how you could be salt and light in the world. What recurring themes have you noticed in Scripture? Among friends? From wise Christians you've read about? At church gatherings?

Now lie down on the floor with your arms outstretched above you, if you can. Ask God what he wants to say to you today. Wait expectantly. Don't be bothered if nothing specific comes to you. Consider this practice as one of the most important things you'll ever do: listening to God and inviting him to speak to you.

PRAY

Talk to God about learning to listen to him. Ask God to show you how he speaks to you most frequently.

LIVE

Sit in the quiet, and lavish yourself with the thought that God seeks you out to speak to you. You get to live an interactive relationship with God.

BEFORE THE THRONE

REVELATION 4:2-8

2-6   I was caught up at once in deep worship and, oh! — a Throne set in Heaven
with One Seated on the Throne, suffused in gem hues of amber and flame
with a nimbus of emerald. Twenty-four thrones circled the Throne, with
Twenty-four Elders seated, white-robed, gold-crowned. Lightning flash
and thunder crash pulsed from the Throne. Seven fire-blazing torches
fronted the Throne (these are the Sevenfold Spirit of God). Before the
Throne it was like a clear crystal sea.

6-8   Prowling around the Throne were Four Animals, all eyes. Eyes to look
ahead, eyes to look behind. The first Animal like a lion, the second like
an ox, the third with a human face, the fourth like an eagle in flight.
The Four Animals were winged, each with six wings. They were all eyes,
seeing around and within. And they chanted night and day, never taking
a break:

> Holy, holy, holy
> Is God our Master, Sovereign-Strong,
> THE WAS, THE IS, THE COMING.

READ

Read the passage once aloud, and get a feel for what is happening. As you read it a second time, do you notice a common theme? Write it down.

THINK/PRAY

Close your eyes and imagine what's described here: the amber and the emerald, the thunder and the lightning, the torches and the sea. See if you can sense the awe of the place. What does it feel like to be there?

Listen as the Four Animals begin to chant, "Holy, holy, holy." Speak these words to God a few times. Share with him what they express for you. Think about what holiness means to you, but not for long. Return your attention to The Was, The Is, The Coming. Join the Four Animals in their worship again: "Holy, holy, holy."

LIVE

What is one way you could worship God today? Perhaps you know a poem or song that puts words and emotion to your love for him today; read it, play it, sing it. Perhaps you have a special skill like dancing, surfing, or art; perform that for him today. Maybe there is a specific action you could take that would honor him. Do it. Maybe you'll want simply to tell him what you like about him.

BEFORE THE THRONE

REVELATION 7:9-12

9-12   I looked again. I saw a huge crowd, too huge to count. Everyone was there—all nations and tribes, all races and languages. And they were *standing*, dressed in white robes and waving palm branches, standing before the Throne and the Lamb and heartily singing:

> Salvation to our God on his Throne!
> Salvation to the Lamb!

All who were standing around the Throne—Angels, Elders, Animals—fell on their faces before the Throne and worshiped God, singing:

> Oh, Yes!
> The blessing and glory and wisdom and thanksgiving,
> The honor and power and strength,
> To our God forever and ever and ever!
> Oh, Yes!

READ

Stand up and read this passage aloud in a loud and excited tone of voice, imagining yourself before the throne of God.

THINK

Have you heard it said that our sole purpose in life is to worship God? Read again the words that the worshipers sing in this scene. How does this relate to your worship of God?

"Salvation to our God." What has God saved you from, specifically?

"The blessing and glory and wisdom and thanksgiving, the honor and power and strength." What comes to mind when you think about these words? What are you feeling about the God described by them? Why?

What might this passage have to do with shared worship in church each week?

PRAY

Why is God worthy of your worship? Consider lying down on your face before him as you tell him (with specifics), just as the angels, elders, and animals do in this passage.

Go on to worship God as you communicate with him. Respond to him with thankfulness, authenticity, honesty, and passion.

LIVE

Take out a piece of paper or your journal. Write down a few sentences or paragraphs telling God how grateful you are for him and for what he has done, is doing, and will do. Include gratitude directed to the Lamb of God. Start and end with the phrase "Oh, yes!"

Then read your writing aloud to God as an act of worship.

DEATH GONE FOR GOOD

REVELATION 21:1-11

1 I saw Heaven and earth new-created. Gone the first Heaven, gone the first earth, gone the sea.

2 I saw Holy Jerusalem, new-created, descending resplendent out of Heaven, as ready for God as a bride for her husband.

3-5 I heard a voice thunder from the Throne: "Look! Look! God has moved into the neighborhood, making his home with men and women! They're his people, he's their God. He'll wipe every tear from their eyes. Death is gone for good — tears gone, crying gone, pain gone — all the first order of things." The Enthroned continued, "Look! I'm making everything new. Write it all down — each word dependable and accurate."

6-8 Then he said, "It's happened. I'm A to Z. I'm the Beginning, I'm the Conclusion. From Water-of-Life Well I give freely to the thirsty. Conquerors inherit all this. I'll be God to them, they'll be sons and daughters to me. But for the rest — the feckless and faithless, degenerates and murderers, sex peddlers and sorcerers, idolaters and all liars — for them it's Lake Fire and Brimstone. Second death!"

9-11 One of the Seven Angels who had carried the bowls filled with the seven final disasters spoke to me: "Come here. I'll show you the Bride, the Wife of the Lamb." He took me away in the Spirit to an enormous, high mountain and showed me Holy Jerusalem descending out of Heaven from God, resplendent in the bright glory of God.

The City shimmered like a precious gem, light-filled, pulsing light.

READ

If you can, skim the expanded passage once quickly to get a broader perspective on the context of these verses. Then read this excerpt three times slowly.

THINK

Among all the images and names given in this passage — for the believers, for God, for the way life will be then and what will happen — which stands out to you? Consider God "mov[ing] into the neighborhood" or God "wip[ing] every tear from [our] eyes." Can you believe that this will someday be reality?

PRAY

Offer God your belief or disbelief in the promise of his coming kingdom. Thank him for the promise of it, even if you struggle to believe. Ask him to help you hope in it. Sit in silence for a bit, and be aware of him hearing you and looking at it all with you.

LIVE

What might be different in you (even if it's just the tiniest shift in perspective), knowing that a place "resplendent in the bright glory of God" waits for you?

DAY 161

GOD ENCOUNTERS

On this seventh day, review and reflect on all you have read this week. Take the time to revel in the ways you've encountered God in the past six days.

LIVING DAILY FOR GOD

Perhaps the beginning of a life lived for him. What was it like? What did you discover that made you stop and really think about this almighty, all-knowing, paradoxical God? What fired your curiosity? What frightened you?

And as he revealed himself to you, how did God work in your life? On the way, what did you discover about him? About yourself? How has he changed who you are to make you more the person he wants you to be?

Take the things you have learned and put into practice and let them become part of the life God has planned for you. Don't let the discipline of reading and studying his Word languish. You're on a roll! Keep up the good work, because God is with you. In the words of the Message, "God, who got you started in this spiritual adventure, shares with us the life of his Son and our Master Jesus. He will never give up on you. Never forget that" (1 Corinthians 1:9).

NOTES

1. C. S. Lewis, *The Lion, the Witch and the Wardrobe* (London: HarperCollins, 1998), 75.
2. Bruce L. Shelley, *Church History in Plain Language* (Nashville: Thomas Nelson, 1995), 3.
3. Oswald Chambers, *My Utmost for His Highest* (Uhrichsville, OH: Barbour, 2006), 52.
4. Teresa of Avila, *Interior Castles: The Collected Works of St. Teresa of Avila,* trans. Kieran Kavanaugh, OCD and Otilio Rodriguez, OCD (Washington, DC: ICS Publications, 1980), 2:309.
5. These questions adapted closely from Emilie Griffin, *Wilderness Time* (San Francisco: HarperSanFrancisco, 1997), 47.
6. Julian of Norwich, *Revelation of Love*, ed. and trans. John Skinner (New York: Doubleday, 1996), 13.
7. *The Book of Common Prayer*, 1983), 337.
8. Margaret Silf, *Going on Retreat* (Chicago: Loyola, 2002), 40–41.
9. Chambers, 193.
10. Bernard of Clairvaux, as quoted in *Prayer: Finding the Heart's True Home* by Richard Foster (San Francisco: HarperSanFrancisco, 1992), 168.
11. Ruth Haley Barton, *Sacred Rhythms* (Downers Grove, IL: InterVarsity, 2006), 117.
12. John Dalrymple, *Simple Prayer* (Wilmington, DE: Michael Glazier, 1984), 109–110.
13. Richard J. Foster, *Prayer: Finding the Heart's True Home* (San Francisco: HarperSanFrancisco, 1992), 61.
14. That the World May Know Ministries "Rabbi and Talmidim," *Follow the Rabbi*, March 7, 2007, http://community.gospelcom.net/Brix?pageID=2753.
15. Douglas V. Steere, *Prayer and Worship* (New York: Edward W. Hazen Foundation, 1938), 34.
16. C. S. Lewis, *The Weight of Glory* (Grand Rapids: Eerdmans, 1965), 14–15.

INDEX

The Message//REMIX: Solo is intended to immerse you in the beauty and depth of the Bible through lectio divina. It is not a topical Bible or a concordance. However, if you are looking for a reading on a specific subject, the following index of topics and day numbers may be of assistance. It is not meant to be an exhaustive list of the topics covered by the Scripture passages discussed in this book. If you find that you want to delve deeper into a particular topic, see *The Message Three-Way Concordance* (Colorado Springs: NavPress, 2006).

ABOUT THE AUTHORS

Eugene H. Peterson is a pastor, scholar, writer, and poet. After teaching at a seminary and then giving nearly thirty years to church ministry in the Baltimore area, he created *The Message* — a vibrant translation of the Bible from the original Greek and Hebrew.

Eugene and his wife, Jan, now live in his native Montana. They are the parents of three and the grandparents of six.

Jan Johnson is a retreat leader and spiritual director and has written more than fifteen books, including *Enjoying the Presence of God* (NavPress), *Savoring God's Word* (NavPress), and *When the Soul Listens* (NavPress).

J.R. Briggs is the pastor and cultural cultivator of *resonate* at Calvary Church in the greater Philadelphia area. He is the author of *When God Says Jump* (TH1NK) and *Redefining Life for Men* (TH1NK). He loves to read, skydive, play basketball, camp, hike, ski, and blog. He and his wife, Megan, live in Perkasie, PA, with their son, Carter.

Katie Peckham has an MA in spiritual formation and soul care from Talbot Seminary and works as a spiritual director in Orange County, CA. She enjoys swimming, running marathons, and teaming up with her husband, Daniel, to serve the Christian missions community by using photojournalism to connect the American church with what God is doing overseas.

Did you enjoy Solo New Testament? Try *The Message//REMIX: Solo* full Bible devotional.

The Message//REMIX: Solo [Full Bible]
Eugene H. Peterson
978-1-60006-105-9

This is not your traditional devotional. This innovative devotional Bible is designed to change how you interact with God's Word and revolves around *lectio divina*, or "divine reading," an ancient approach to exploring Scripture updated for today's Bible reader. Each devotion delivers a unique, contemplative study that will encourage you to Read, Think, Pray, and Live God's Word every day. *Solo* also includes a topical index and a numbered devotion so you can start any day of the year.

To order copies, call NavPress at 1-800-366-7788, or log on to www.navpress.com.

Join NavPress in the fight against Breast Cancer
The all new *Message//REMIX: Solo [Pink Edition]*

The Message//REMIX: Solo [Pink Edition]
Eugene H. Peterson
978-1-60006-869-0

One in eight women will be diagnosed with breast cancer, a disease that takes the lives of more than forty thousand women a year. *The Message// REMIX: Solo [Pink Edition]* offers daily encouragement and hope during these tough times. Through the approach of lectio divina, or "divine reading," each devotion offers you support and encouragement. A portion of the proceeds from each edition sold will be donated toward finding a cure for breast cancer.

To order copies, call NavPress at 1-800-366-7788,
or log on to www.navpress.com.